:: CONTENT

Enter ↵

This guide supports Books 1 to 4 of How to Code. It is intended to be used by parents, teachers or other adults who are helping children learn to code.

How to use this book

PAGE-BY-PAGE GUIDES

While children are exploring coding with Books 1 to 4, you can keep track of their learning with our page-by-page guides. You'll find explanations of the **Key concepts** covered. Where some concepts may be hard to understand, these pages give you **Extra help** on how to explain them. It also lists **Common confusions** that children may experience and ways to overcome them. When children have found ideas easy to grasp, the **Taking it further** sections provide extra challenges.

EXTENSION PROJECTS

For each of Books 1 to 4, you will find a number of fun extension projects that will reinforce the key concepts learnt and take children's learning even deeper.

TECHNICAL GUIDES

At the back of the book are technical guides to the five languages covered in this series: **Logo**, **Scratch**, **Python**, **HTML** (Hyper Text Mark-up Language) and **JavaScript**. Here you'll find all the information you need to get hold of, use and troubleshoot these languages.

APPENDICES

The **Language comparison** section will help you understand the differences and similarities between each of the languages covered in this series. The **Progression statements** will allow children to recognize their own progress and identify their next steps for learning. You will also find a **Glossary** and all the **Answers** to the challenges set in this book.

Learning to code

Each of the four books in this series covers a number of key concepts, such as loops, variables and selection. The concepts grow in complexity as you progress from book to book. Each book uses two coding languages to help children think more deeply about these key concepts.

All children learn at different rates. Some children will struggle with particular ideas and find other parts of coding easy. It is important to let them progress at a rate that gives them time to explore and really embed their learning.

Many children will be happy to spend several hours on a computer or tablet. This is not recommended! It is important to take a break and do something else at regular intervals. While coding is a very important skill for the future, many of the key concepts can be learnt and reinforced away from the computer. The higher-level skills of problem-solving and breaking down solutions into parts can be developed equally well by the use of construction toys and creative play.

Even if you are not a coding expert yourself, ask children to explain to you how to code the activity they are working on — and don't be afraid to have a go yourself. Most importantly, let children explore and have fun with their coding.

Book 1

Book 1 introduces children to the idea that computers need to be given instructions to tell them what to do. Children learn that **commands** need to be clear and precise, and given in the correct sequence, if the computer is going to do what they want. A number of activities are offered that will help teach these ideas, initially without using a computer.

Two computer languages are then introduced. The first, **Logo**, is used to introduce children to typing simple instructions that get an instant result. As they type commands, the onscreen turtle moves and draws, encouraging them to experiment. The second language, **Scratch**, takes these ideas further and introduces children to **inputs**. Children learn to program a simple game that uses inputs: pressing keys will move the Scratch sprite around the screen.

ISBN 978 1 78493 236 7

Book 2

The second book in the series starts off by explaining one of the key concepts in coding – the use of **loops** and repetition. Using **Logo** and then **Scratch**, children are shown how they can use loops to draw simple shapes, and then to build them into interesting patterns. They find out how loops can have conditions attached to them, so they will loop until a particular event occurs – such as one sprite catching another in a game.

The use of outputs other than the screen is explored via the use of **sound**. Children learn how to create a basic piano or synthesizer program. Next, **variables** are used to show children how programs store and change data, such as the score in a game. Children will build their own games and activities to practise these skills in Scratch.

ISBN 978 1 78493 237 4

Book 3

The concept of **selection** is explored in Book 3, using **Scratch** to build a quiz. Children develop this idea further by combining selection with variables to add point scoring to their quiz. They also create a game in which points are scored for each apple their sprite 'eats'.

Book 3 then takes these concepts into a professional coding environment, using the **Python** language. Children learn how to enter commands using a special text editor and create their own programs in Python. They find out how to use programming **libraries** to generate **random numbers** and produce **graphics**.

ISBN 978 1 78493 238 1

Book 4

The final book in the series takes a look at the **World Wide Web** and how it works, including **URLs (Uniform Resource Locators)** and **hyperlinks**. Children learn to create web pages using **HTML (Hyper Text Mark-up Language)** and a text editor. They find out how to add different objects or elements to a page using **tags**, and how to link pages together.

Book 4 then shows children how they can add **JavaScript** coding to a page. While HTML is the language used to code what is on a web page, JavaScript is used to code what a web page does. Children learn how JavaScript handles loops and how they can create their own **functions**. They explore how web pages can include images and buttons, and how code can be linked to them.

ISBN 978 1 78493 239 8

PAGES 6–7
Giving instructions

  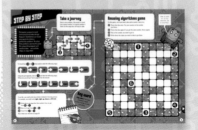

OBJECTIVES

The first step towards becoming a good programmer is to learn that computers need clear and precise instructions to make things happen. 'Giving instructions' offers a number of activities to help children learn this concept, before they start work at the computer. By taking it in turns to 'be a robot', children will understand that it is essential to have a clear idea about what you want a program to do before you start coding.

KEY CONCEPTS: PRECISION AND SEQUENCE

We need to make sure children understand that commands must be precise. It is no good saying 'move' in a computer program – we need to tell the computer which object and which direction.

The next thing we need to do is ensure that any commands we give a program are in the correct order. This is something that we can demonstrate quite easily by mixing up the order of instructions and seeing what happens.

PAGES 8–9
Step by step

OBJECTIVES

In 'Step by step', children will learn the term 'algorithm'. An algorithm is explained as the steps a program needs to take in order to solve a problem. In the game on page 9, children write down the sequence of steps they need to take to get from one place on the board to another. This is a basic algorithm.

TAKING IT FURTHER

As children become more experienced programmers, their definition of 'algorithm' will need to become more sophisticated. Once they progress beyond simple programming, their code may branch off in different directions, or respond to different inputs. At this point, they will not be using a straightforward sequence of commands or steps, so it may be more helpful to think about an algorithm as being a set of rules to solve a problem or make a game work. As they progress further, they will start to create programs that have a number of different algorithms at work.

EXTRA HELP

It can be very effective to write down instructions on separate cards. Then you and your children can re-arrange them.

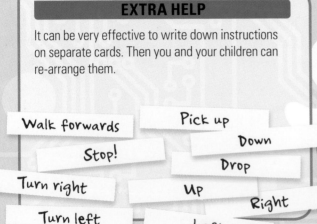

Walk forwards
Pick up
Down
Stop!
Drop
Turn right
Up
Right
Turn left
Left

PAGES 10–11
Coded messages

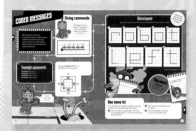

OBJECTIVES

Here children will learn that the instructions we give to computers need to have more information and be precise. Rather than just telling a robot to move up, we introduce the idea that we can use instructions like **U5** to move up 5 squares. This idea is developed further to create simple programs, such as **U4 R4 D4 L4**, that can be used to draw a square.

TAKING IT FURTHER

In the game 'You name it!', on page 11, children will write programs to spell out their name or initials. If children want to take the game further, ask them to invent some new commands to change the colour of what they are going to draw. They might choose to use **PR** to mean 'pen – red' or **PY** to mean 'pen – yellow'. Use these new commands to create longer programs or even whole words.

For example, the following program would write 'elsa':

PR (pen red) **R3 U2 L3 D3 R4**

PB (pen blue) **U5 D5 R1**

PG (pen green) **R3 U2 L3 U1 R3**

PO (pen orange) **R4 D3 L3 U2 R3**

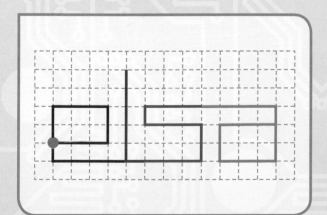

PAGES 12–13
Spinning around

OBJECTIVES

To move a robot around the floor, or a turtle around the screen, we need to use commands to move it forward by a certain amount, or rotate it by a number of degrees. This page explains how degrees are used to measure how far things are rotated. To keep things simple, for now we are using only 'quarter-turns' of 90 degrees.

When we need to explain how big things are on a computer screen, we usually measure in pixels. Each dot on a computer screen is a pixel (short for 'picture element'). If children are having trouble grasping what a pixel is, you can demonstrate by using a strong magnifying glass to look at a computer screen, or by zooming into a low-quality digital photograph. As you keep zooming in, the picture will become blurry or 'blocky' and the individual pixels will be apparent.

TAKING IT FURTHER

Play 'human robots'. Instead of using squared paper, work outside on some paving stones or in the playground. Ask children to work with a partner. One child will give instructions, and the other will be a robot carrying them out. The robot partner can use chalk to draw on the ground as they carry out the instructions.

PAGES 14–15
Learning Logo

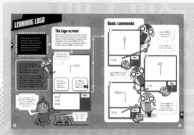

OBJECTIVES
Here children will learn the basics of a simple programming language: Logo. They will do their first basic coding. Children will start programming an onscreen turtle (arrow) with three basic commands: move forward, turn left and turn right. For a technical guide to using Logo, turn to page 50 of this book.

COMMON CONFUSIONS
Some children find it hard to work out whether to turn the turtle left or right, particularly when the turtle is facing downwards. A good way to support them is to make a small paper turtle that children can turn to face the same direction as the turtle on the screen.

PAGES 16–17
Logo shapes

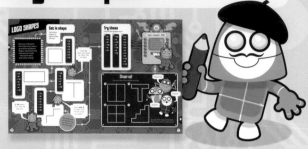

OBJECTIVES
Now that children have learnt to move the turtle around on the Logo screen, they will learn to write more purposeful programs to draw particular shapes.

TAKING IT FURTHER
If children are ready to take their Logo programming to the next level, ask them to:

1. Design a simple pattern and create it using Logo. Write down the code and share it with a partner so they can make the pattern.

2. Make a poster for younger children explaining how to use Logo.

3. Play 'human robots' with a partner, using Logo commands. Give your partner commands to move around the playground while drawing shapes with a piece of chalk.

4. Draw some of the letters in your name using Logo commands. Write down the commands that you use. Make sure you use only horizontal and vertical lines for now.

For example, the following program would write 'A':

```
fd 100 rt 90 fd 50 rt 90
fd 50 rt 90 fd 50 rt 180
fd 50 rt 90 fd 50
```

Starting Scratch

TRY IT OUT

OBJECTIVES

Here children will learn the basics of the Scratch programming language. Scratch is a good next step after Logo. It enables children to grasp more complex coding ideas, but it is still very simple to use. For a technical guide to using Scratch, turn to page 52 of this book.

EXTRA HELP

Before children start programming with Scratch, you can give them a demonstration of how it works. Start by showing them the different groups of code blocks (such as Events and Motion). Follow this by demonstrating how code blocks can be dragged to the scripts area (on the right of the screen) and joined up to make short programs. Show them how each code block can be run by clicking it. Let them see how code blocks can be removed from a program by dragging them out of the scripts area, and how blocks can be separated by dragging the bottom block downwards.

TAKING IT FURTHER

If children are ready to try more, ask them to:

1 Drag the sprite to the left of the screen. Make it move all the way to the right by clicking **'Move 10 steps'** in the **Motion** group. How many times do you need to click it? Check the answer on page 62.

2 Change the number of steps the sprite moves each time you click it. In order to cross the screen in 5 clicks, what number do you need to change it to? What number makes it cross the screen in 2 clicks? How many steps do you think it is across the whole screen? Check the answers on page 62.

Pen down

OBJECTIVES

In 'Pen down', children will learn to draw all sorts of shapes and patterns using Scratch. The **Pen** group gives children access to the **'Pen up'** and **'Pen down'** commands. After allowing some time for experimentation, encourage children to plan the programs they will be creating in rough before they start.

TAKING IT FURTHER

Ask children to have a go at these exercises:

1 Write simple programs to draw each of the digits 1, 2 and 3. There are several different ways to draw these numbers. For one possible solution, turn to page 62.

2 Drag the programs together to make a longer program that writes 123.

3 Work with a partner. Draw a simple shape for them on a piece of paper. Only use horizontal and vertical lines. Use squared paper if you can. Challenge your partner to draw the pattern using Scratch.

PAGES 22–23
Press a key

OBJECTIVES

'Press a key' teaches two key concepts: inputs and events. Children will learn that inputs and events are vital to creating almost all games and more sophisticated programs. Children will also begin to develop their thinking about what programming means. Very basic programming is about following a single sequence of commands. However, when we start using inputs and events, programs will respond by following different sequences of commands.

KEY CONCEPTS: INPUTS AND EVENTS

An input is an action – such as pressing a key – that tells a computer to do something. We will learn that, instead of our code working in the same way each time the program is run, different parts of the program will be followed when different inputs occur. In the example on pages 22–23, pressing 'R' will run Scratch code to make the sprite move right. Pressing 'L' will run a different bit of code, which will make the sprite move left.

Programmers call an input action, such as a key press, an event. Other events might be something being clicked with a mouse, or the program starting.

At this point, it may be worth revisiting what an algorithm is – we are starting to move on from our original definition of it being the 'steps to solve a problem' (see Book 1 pages 8–9) and more towards it being the 'set of rules' to describe how a game or program works.

PAGES 24–25
Inputs and directions

OBJECTIVES

Children will learn to make the Scratch sprite move in different directions by pressing different keys. These exercises are a progression from those in 'Press a key' on the previous pages. Children will need a very basic understanding of degrees (see Book 1 pages 12–13).

EXTRA HELP

To carry out these exercises, children will need to use the **'Point in direction'** code block, which gives directions in degrees. To keep things simple, we are only going to work with the angles 0, 90, 180, 270 and 360 degrees. The **'Point in direction'** block also offers a pull-down menu that gives reminders, such as '90° (right)'. Scratch uses -90° to point left – again, there is a reminder that this means left in the pull-down menu.

TAKING IT FURTHER

If children want to go further, ask them to write lots of short, simple programs (answers are on page 62):

1. Make a simple program that moves the sprite up, down, left and right when the **cursor keys** are pressed instead of 'U', 'D', 'L', 'R'.

2. Make a program that moves the sprite a big distance when **'B'** is pressed and a small one when **'S'** is pressed.

3. Make a program that moves the sprite diagonally when the **space bar** is pressed.

Sketching with inputs

Debugging

OBJECTIVES

Children will create their own drawing game using Scratch. This exercise offers plenty of opportunities to practise using inputs and a lot of scope to take ideas further. Once children have got a basic version of their drawing program working, you could talk to them about how computers use numbers to represent colours.

TAKING IT FURTHER

Children can try adding these extra features to their game:

1. Add a **'When key pressed'** block from the **Events** group and a **'Clear'** block from the **Pen** group, so the artist can clear the screen with a key press.

2. Add another set of blocks so the artist can lift the pen up when **'U'** is pressed.

3. Add another set of blocks so the artist can start drawing again when **'P'** is pressed.

4. Add more blocks (using the **Events** and **Motion** groups) so the artist can draw diagonally.

5. Experiment with setting the pen colour (using the **Pen** group) and use your findings to make a table. Write the colour names in one column and the value to set pen colour to in the next column.

Check the answers on page 62.

OBJECTIVES

Children will learn the meaning of 'debugging' and practise fixing some simple mistakes in Logo and Scratch codes. Debugging is an essential skill to develop. However, prevention is better than cure, so these pages also offer guidelines about planning and testing short programs.

EXTRA HELP

When teaching children how to debug, it is very useful to model and demonstrate the process. For example, make a simple program that moves a sprite in Scratch. Change a small part of it so that it doesn't work or the sprite moves in the wrong direction. Ask children if they can work out what is wrong. If you are working with a group, ask successful debuggers to explain how they fixed the code, so they can model this approach for everyone else.

COMMON CONFUSIONS

A common confusion at this level of coding is which way is left and which is right when moving around an upside-down sprite. To help, make a simple sprite or triangle out of a small piece of paper (see page 8 of this book).

TIP

Sometimes it may be easier for children to start again rather than debug code that they cannot fix. Get them to plan or explain carefully what they want their code to do, and to rebuild and test it gradually. Make sure they plan realistically. Start with simple games or programs, then build up.

Drawing Scratch graphics

As children become more proficient coders, they will enjoy creating their own graphics to use in their programs. This will encourage them to be more inventive and to unleash their imaginations. Here is a guide to creating graphics in Scratch.

KEY TECHNIQUES TO LEARN

Although we can draw images on computers in a similar way to drawing on paper, there are some important differences. Learning about these differences will help you create better images to use in your programs. You can practise the techniques on this page by using the sprite editor in Scratch. You could also use a program such as Microsoft Paint if you are using a Windows PC, or a more complex package such as Adobe Photoshop. Any images you create can be saved and used in your code.

UNDO

When we make a mistake drawing with a pencil, we can use a rubber to erase what went wrong. Although there is a rubber in most painting programs, it is usually much better to click the **'Undo'** button straight away (or **'Edit'** then **'Undo'**) after making a mistake. **'Undo'** will take away the last thing you did.

ZOOM IN AND ZOOM OUT

It can be hard to draw things accurately with a mouse. It is much easier if you zoom in to make everything look larger when you are trying to make things line up or get something in the right place. When you have finished working on something, zoom out again to get a view of the overall image.

Or use the Select tool.

MOVE THINGS AROUND

On a piece of paper, if we draw something in the wrong place we have to rub it out and draw it again. On a computer, we can move it to the correct place. If you have just drawn a shape, there may be handles to move or resize it. If not, use the **Select** tool to draw round part of your picture and drag it to where you need it.

Use the Line, Ellipse and Rectangle tools.

BUILD IMAGES WITH SHAPES

Although you can draw anything with a brush, it is often easier to build up a digital picture from a series of shapes. Lines will be straighter and curves will be smoother. Try working with the **Ellipse** tool for drawing details such as wheels, eyes, heads, bodies, flowers and rockets! Why not experiment with the **Rectangle** tool for drawing cars, buildings, walls, roads, teeth, robots and trees.

Use the Select tool.

CUT UP SHAPES

If you can't find or draw the shape you need, break up another one. For example, draw an oval with the **Ellipse** tool, then use the **Select** tool to choose the top part of it. Drag it off the screen and you're left with a smile!

Draw a rocket

Using the techniques shown opposite, create a rocket to use as a sprite in a
Scratch program, such as the **Space Game** on the following pages.

1

In Scratch, start by clicking
'Paint new sprite'.

2

Select the **Ellipse** tool.

 Set to fill in. Choose red.

Now draw a wide ellipse.

3

Use the **Select** tool to draw a box
round one end. Drag the end off
the drawing area to remove it.
Repeat for the other end.

4

Zoom in. In a darker colour, use
the **Line** tool to draw a pointed
rocket tip.

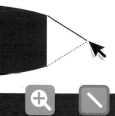

5

Use the **Fill** tool to colour in the
rocket tip, then zoom out.

6

Draw another ellipse, then chop
off one end with the **Select** tool.

7

Use the **Select** tool to draw
round the top half and drag it off,
making a rocket fin.

8

Do the same with the other side.

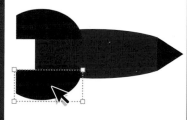

9

Decorate your rocket with
the **Ellipse**, **Rectangle** and
Line tools.

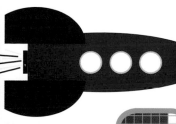

Your picture
will be stored
as pixels.

Practise these
techniques to make
your own fabulous
sprites. Use them in
your own programs.

Space game

This activity shows children how they can create games that include their own graphics. It also builds on all the Scratch skills learnt in Book 1. This Space Game uses a drawn rocket and background image. The rocket will fly when different keys are pressed. One key will make the rocket fly straight, and two other keys will make the rocket turn left or right. Once children have built this game, encourage them to plan their own simple game, create the graphics and code it!

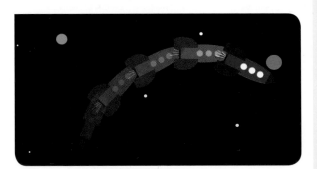

1

Start Scratch. Delete the main sprite by right-clicking on it and then choosing **'Delete'**. (On a Mac, you'll need to hold the **'Control'** key when you click the sprite.)

2

Now draw your own rocket sprite, like the one on page 13.

Right-clicking means click the button on the right side of the mouse.

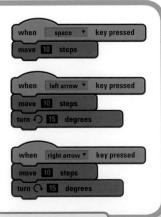

3

Now we need to add some code to make the rocket move forward, and to turn left and right.

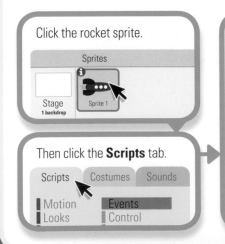

Click the rocket sprite.

Then click the **Scripts** tab.

Drag three **'When key pressed'** blocks from the **Events** group.

Drag the **'Move'** and **'Turn'** blocks from the **Motion** group.

Choose the keys you want to use to make the rocket move forward and turn left and right.

  SPACE BAR

4

Now draw your own background picture for the game.

First, click **'Stage'**.

Then click **'Backdrops'**.

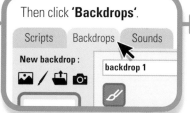

Click the **Fill** tool and choose the black colour.

Now click the background to colour it in.

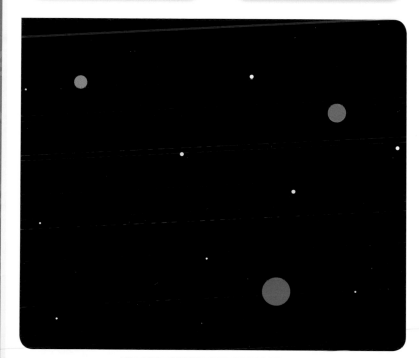

Use the **Brush** tool to draw some stars.

Use the **Line width** slider to change the size of the stars.

Use the **Ellipse** tool to draw some planets. Hold down the **'Shift'** key to make perfect circles.

Click this button to make your program as big as the screen!

Saving your code

To save your work, click the **'File'** menu (top left of screen), then click **'Download to your computer'**.

To get your work back another day, first you need to open up Scratch on your browser. Then click the **'File'** menu and choose **'Upload from your computer'**.

PAGES 6–7
Loops

OBJECTIVES

One of the key concepts in any programming language is the use of loops to repeat instructions over and over again. In these exercises, children will learn to use Logo to program simple loops that will draw shapes.

KEY CONCEPT: LOOPS

Before moving to the computer, talk to children about how we use loops in everyday life, and get them to think of some examples. How about walking to school every day (repeating 5 times) or putting on shoes (repeating 2 times)? Explain that using repetition is a way of making instructions more efficient. Discuss the idea of telling a millipede to put on each of its shoes one at a time – or using a repeat loop. Get children to write down some instructions, for example:

Tell a 300-legged millipede to put on its shoes:
repeat 300 [put on shoe]

Tell a pupil to walk to school every day:
repeat 5 [walk to school]

EXTRA HELP

If children are unable to visualize the shapes while doing the 'Coding simple loops' exercises, get them to read the commands out loud. They could even go outside with a piece of chalk and a partner. One child could read aloud the commands while the other becomes a 'human robot' – drawing on the ground while obeying the repeated commands. Note also that, when programming Logo loops, children may forget to type both brackets, or they may type curly brackets instead of square ones.

PAGES 8–9
Patterns with loops

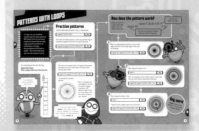

OBJECTIVES

These exercises will take children's understanding of loops to the next level. We will explore the power of running one loop inside another loop. We will use this concept to make a pattern in Logo.

KEY CONCEPT: LOOP INSIDE A LOOP

This can be a difficult concept to explain to children, so it will be helpful to use a fun analogy before moving to the computer. Imagine that a family of four 300-legged millipedes are getting ready to put their shoes on. Let's write down some commands to get them ready, using a loop within a loop:

repeat 4 [repeat 300 [put on shoe]]

Remind children that they need to put square brackets around the commands they are repeating. As there are two loops, there will need to be two left and two right brackets.

TAKING IT FURTHER

Using Logo, ask children to type this code:

repeat 20 [repeat 4 [fd 100 rt 90] rt 5]

The code will not draw a complete pattern. Experiment with different values for the first repeat to complete the pattern. The answer is on page 62.

PAGES 10–11
Loops in Scratch

PAGES 12–13
Loops forever

OBJECTIVES

Children will now learn to create loops in Scratch. Scratch works in a similar way to Logo, making it straightforward to apply what has already been learnt. Trying out loops in another programming language will help children to focus on the concept of repetition. Discuss with children the similarities and differences in creating a simple loop in the two languages.

TAKING IT FURTHER

1 Show this code to children and ask them to predict what it will draw. (It's an octagon.)

2 Ask children to change the code to draw a 12-sided shape (a dodecagon).

Most children will work out that they need to change the number of repeats to 12 in order to draw a 12-sided shape. Most children will find it harder to work out what angle they need to turn. Get them to experiment with using larger or smaller values.

The correct angle to turn is 30 degrees. This is because, in order to complete the shape, we need to turn 360 degrees in total. We are doing this in 12 steps, so 360 degrees divided by 12 gives us 30 degrees.

OBJECTIVES

So far, we have looked at loops that run a specific number of times. Now children will learn to use loops that run forever – or until the program is stopped. They will use a 'forever' loop to code a swimming fish in Scratch. Children can discuss the idea that most games need a 'main loop' that keeps running all the time. A main loop can do things like move objects or sprites around the screen.

TAKING IT FURTHER

If children are ready to learn more about 'forever' loops, ask them to carry out these exercises:

1 Discuss what would happen if, instead of using a 'forever' loop for our swimming fish, we used a 'repeat 100' loop. (The game would stop after a few seconds.)

2 Using a 'forever' loop, make another game in Scratch, this time with a plane that flies around the screen.

3 Design your own game in which an object moves around the screen following the mouse. Let your imagination run riot!

PAGES 14–15
Repeat until...

OBJECTIVES

Children will learn to use 'repeat until' loops in Scratch. Most games that use loops will need to stop running at some point: for example, when a car crashes into a wall.

KEY CONCEPT: 'REPEAT UNTIL' LOOPS

Before children start coding, it is worth talking about the idea of repeating a task until something happens. For example:

Repeat [eat your peas] until none left
Repeat [pour water into glass] until full

PAGES 16–17
Repeat until caught

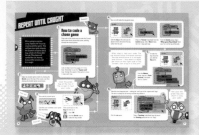

OBJECTIVES

Using Scratch, children will program a chasing game using another 'repeat until' loop. In this program, children will learn to code a second sprite, and the loop will repeat until the two sprites are touching.

COMMON CONFUSIONS

Programming a second sprite can be fiddly. Children will need to follow the instructions carefully. Make sure that the cat and dog each get the right bit of code. There are two different 'mini-programs' or loops running here – one for each sprite. To change the code for a sprite, make sure that sprite is clicked first!

EXTRA HELP

Children may not have come across coordinates before, or used the terms x and y to describe where things are located on a screen. If so, show children the diagram below. Explain that the green dot is positioned at x=3 and y=2. The red dot is at x=6 and y=4. Ask them to work out x and y for the other dots.

When we use **'Set x to'** or **'Set y to'** in Scratch, we are setting the position of the sprite using x and y values. We could move the sprite to the blue dot with this code:

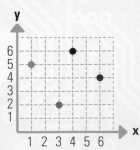

PAGES 18–19
Adding sound

OBJECTIVES

In 'Adding sound', we introduce using sound as an output within coding. Using Scratch, we will code a tune and create a piano program. The Scratch **'Play note'** command needs two values. The first controls the pitch of the note, and the second how long the note lasts.

TAKING IT FURTHER

After children have completed the piano program, they could add some new key press events to change the instrument. Each of these will use the **'Set instrument'** code block. Now let them experiment!

PAGES 20–21
Sound effects

OBJECTIVES

Children will extend their ability to code with sound by looking at how sound can be added into games and other programs. The exercises on these pages combine playing sounds with loops. Children will also use sound files that have been recorded, such as a meowing cat for the chasing game in Book 2 pages 16–17.

TAKING IT FURTHER

Children can record their own sound files in Scratch. You need a built-in microphone on the computer or an external one. Make sure microphones are set up correctly.

1 To add your own recorded sound, drag a **'Play sound'** code block onto the scripts area and click **'Record'**.

2 Click the **'Record'** button and create your sound. Then click **'Stop'**.

3 Click the **'Scripts'** tab.

4 Click **'Recording1'** to select your recording, then click the **'Play sound'** block.

Try putting this **'Play sound'** block in a program.

PAGES 22–23
Variables

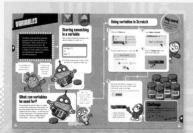

OBJECTIVES

These pages explain variables, which are a key concept in any programming language. Before moving on to more complex exercises on the following pages, children will grasp the idea of variables by creating a simple program using a single variable in Scratch.

KEY CONCEPT: VARIABLES

Variables are a way that computer programs store pieces of data or information. Unlike normal numbers, variables can change their value when something happens. Although variables can seem like quite an abstract idea, children will be familiar with the use of a score variable in games. They will be used to the idea that the value of the score in a game can change from being zero at the start — and will increase as the game progresses.

COMMON CONFUSIONS

Some children may be confused by the difference between the letter a, the variable a and the value of the variable a. This is how Scratch handles variables:

This just means: display the letter a. In many other programming languages, it would have speech marks round it – "a" – and be called a string.

This means: display the value of the variable a. In our code it looks like an a but when we run the code, it shows up as the value in a.

PAGES 24–25
Keeping score

OBJECTIVES

Using Scratch, children will learn to create a score variable (called s) for a game. The variable will keep track of how long the game is running. At the start of the game, the value of s is set to 0. Every time the main loop in the game repeats, the value of the variable s (our score) goes up by 1.

COMMON CONFUSIONS

It is important that children understand the difference between setting a variable to a specific value, and increasing it. Try swapping round the **'Set s to 0'** and **'Change s by 1'** code blocks to demonstrate what happens.

TAKING IT FURTHER

When children are ready to try more, ask them to:

1 Change the shark game to make the score go up in 2s, 5s or 10s. Then check the answers on page 62.

2 Use a **'Say'** code block to display the score at the end of the game.

PAGES 26–27
Counting clicks

OBJECTIVES

This project will extend children's understanding of variables: instead of having a score that is increased in the main repeat loop, the score will increase when the sprite is clicked. This project also recaps on working with loops and coordinates.

HOW THE CODE WORKS

```
1   when        clicked
2   set x to    -180
3   set  s ▼ to 0
4   repeat until   touching   edge ▼  ?
5       move   5   steps
                              ↵
6   say   s


7   when this sprite clicked
8   change   s ▼ by   1
```

❶ Start the program.

❷ Move the cat sprite to the left of the screen.

❸ Reset the score to 0.

❹ Repeat the commands in the loop until the sprite reaches the edge of the screen.

❺ Move the sprite.

❻ Show the score (if the program breaks out of the loop because the sprite reaches the edge).

❼ When the sprite is clicked...

❽ Make the score go up.

PAGES 28–29
Debugging

OBJECTIVES

These pages will teach children the vital skill of debugging, while consolidating their knowledge of loops and variables. Now children are writing longer programs, they will be experiencing more bugs and need to develop their skills to fix them. These pages also offer tips on avoiding bugs in the first place.

TIP

One skill to start developing at this point is the ability to look through some code and see what each line does. Saying each line out loud, or to a partner, can really help. The act of explaining each line can allow children to check that what they want to happen is what the program is being told to do.

This technique is used by professional programmers – in a quite surprising way. There is an established technique called 'rubber duck debugging'. Programmers look through any code that doesn't work, and explain what each line does out loud... to a rubber duck!

Maybe one day the duck will learn to code too!

Racing game

This project will extend children's learning by combining a 'repeat until' loop with a variable. Using Scratch, we will create a car-racing game in which the loop will keep the car moving until it hits something. A variable will be used to time how long the car has been driven without crashing.

1

Start Scratch. Delete the main sprite by right-clicking on it and then choosing **'Delete'**. (On a Mac, you will need to hold the **'Control'** key while you click.)

2

Now draw your own car sprite.

Start by clicking **'Paint new sprite'**.

Choose a colour and select the **Rectangle** tool. Draw the car body.

Then add more rectangles, wheels and a driver (using the **Ellipse** tool).

4

Now draw your own track for the car to drive on. Don't make it too narrow.

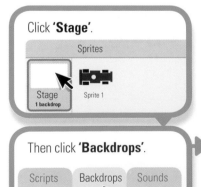

Click **'Stage'**.

Then click **'Backdrops'**.

3

Make the car sprite smaller by clicking the **Shrink** icon and then clicking the car several times.

Click the **Fill** tool and choose a green colour. Now click the background to colour it in. Then use grey rectangles to draw the track.

5

Now we need to make the car move until it goes off the track.

Click **Sprite1** to make sure we are adding code to the car sprite. Then click on the **'Scripts'** tab.

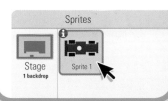

Drag all of these code blocks onto the scripts area.

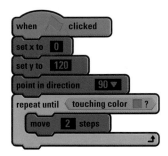

You need to set the **'Touching color'** code block to the green of your grass. Click on the coloured square, then click on the grass on the stage area.

Click the green flag icon near the top of the Scratch screen to test your code.

If the car doesn't move to the track when you click the flag, adjust the **'Set x to'** and **'Set y to'** values. The **'Point in direction'** block will make it drive to the right.

6

Add two **'When key pressed'** blocks from the **Events** group to steer the car. Test your code and try pressing the arrow keys.

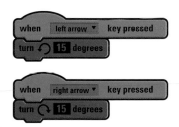

Click this button to make the game larger!

7

Now make a variable to keep the score.

Choose the **Data** group.

Click **'Make a variable'**.

Call it 's' (for score).

Then click **'OK'**.

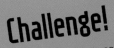

8

Drop a **'Set s to 0'** code block in at the start of the game.

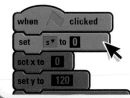

9

Drop a **'Change s by 1'** code block in the main repeat loop to make the score go up.

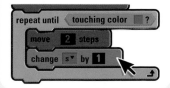

Challenge!

Can you add sound effects so you get a crash at the end (try a drum sound)?

Fun with variables

Once children have got to grips with variables and are using them confidently, there are lots of ways to extend their understanding. Here we will use Scratch to combine variables with loops, sound and graphics.

VARIABLES AND SOUND

Try out this program, which combines a loop with a variable as well as sounds.

1 From the **Control** group, drag a **'Repeat'** loop block over to the scripts area.

2 Add a **'Play note'** code block from the **Sound** group.

3 Click the **Data** group and make a variable called 'a'.

> Data
> Make a Variable

4 Put a **'Set a to 0'** code block before the loop starts. Set 'a' to 60.

```
set    a▼ to  60
repeat  10
    change  a▼ by  1
    play note  a  for  0.5  beats
```

Drag over the small circle with **'a'** in it and drop it in the **'Play note'** code block.

Drop a **'Change a by 1'** code block into the repeat loop. Test your code. Experiment!

Now create these 3 programs. What sort of games would they create useful sound effects for?

```
set instrument to  17▼
set  a▼ to  60
repeat  12
    play note  a  for  0.1  beats
    change  a▼ by  5
repeat  10
    play note  a  for  0.1  beats
    change  a▼ by  -5
```
Use two loops.

```
set volume to  100 %
set  a▼ to  100
repeat  10
    set volume to  a  %
    play note  60▼ for  0.1  beats
    change  a▼ by  -10
```
Create an echo.

```
set instrument to  16▼
set  a▼ to  100
repeat  20
    play note  a  for  0.05  beats
    change  a▼ by  -5
```
Experiment with the amount 'a' changes by and how many times to repeat loops.

Variables and graphics

Now that you have learnt to create basic graphic patterns with a loop, try adding variables. It is possible to create some interesting effects by using a variable within a loop to change things such as how long the shape's sides are. When drawing in Scratch, remember to shrink the cat sprite so it doesn't get in the way.

1

This loop makes a square:

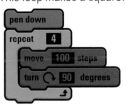

Now add a variable to make a spiral:

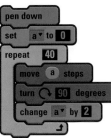

Can you explain how this loop works?

The square program has a fixed side length of 100 steps.

The spiral works by increasing the side length by 2 steps each loop and storing the length in a variable called 'a'.

Now try experimenting with the angle that is turned, or the amount 'a' changes.

2

This program draws a thick line:

A variable makes the line get thicker and thicker:

3

This program changes the colour as well as the pen size. When setting the pen colour, make sure you use the **'Set pen color to 0'** block.

Now try playing around with different ways that variables can change what is drawn.

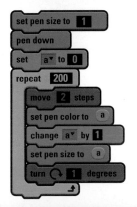

PAGES 6–7
'If' commands

PAGES 8–9
Quiz time

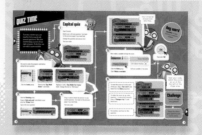

OBJECTIVES

'If commands' introduces a concept called selection. Selection allows a program to run different bits of code in response to a question or input. Using Scratch, children will code a question-and-answer program using selection.

OBJECTIVES

Children will extend their understanding of selection by programming a quiz in Scratch. This project also uses a variable to count the score.

KEY CONCEPT: SELECTION

When children start coding, most of their programs will run in the same way each time, following a sequence of commands, one after the other. This is called sequential code.
For example:

start

move forward 10 steps

turn right

move forward 10 steps

stop

Selection means that a program may branch off and run a different piece of code in response to something happening, such as a question being answered. For example:

start

ask 5 x 5 ?

does the user type 25?

say 'Well Done!'

stop   stop

Programmers often call this a 'conditional statement'.

EXTRA HELP

Children may need a reminder of how to use variables, which were introduced in Book 2 of this series. Variables are a way that computer programs store pieces of data or information. Unlike normal numbers, variables can change their value when something happens. Although variables can seem like quite an abstract idea, children will quickly grasp the concept of using a variable to keep a score. Most children are already familiar with how a score starts at zero at the beginning of a game – and increases as the game progresses.

Make sure children understand the difference between setting the score at the start of the quiz, and adding 1 to it when they get an answer correct. Explain that by putting **'Change s by 1'** inside the 'C' shaped part of the **'If then'** block, it only runs if the answer is correct.

OBJECTIVES

'Else commands' continues our work on selection. Children will learn how to use 'if then else' commands in Scratch. A basic 'if' code block allows us to do something if a condition is true – for example, to show 'Well done!' if an answer is correct. Adding an 'else' part to the code block allows us to run a different bit of code if the answer is wrong.

EXTRA HELP

Move away from the computer to play these fun games that demonstrate the concept of 'if then else'. These exercises will also enable you to see whether children have understood the key concept of selection or not.

Ask these questions, or type the questions on a computer (using a large font or projector):

if your age equals 10 **then** stand up **else** sit down

if you have black hair **then** wave your hands **else** pat your stomach

if you are a girl **then** dance **else** put your fingers in your ears

Or give each child a playing card and ask questions such as:

if card = 5 **then** wave **else** frown

if card = red **then** jump up and down **else** put your hands on your head

OBJECTIVES

This project will combine children's understanding of selection with their knowledge of loops. Loops are covered in Book 2 of this series – turn to page 16 of this book for a recap. In this apple-eating game, a 'forever' loop keeps our cat sprite moving towards the mouse pointer. An 'if then' command will make apple sprites disappear if they are touched (or eaten!) by the cat.

TAKING IT FURTHER

If children are comfortable with both selection and loops, they could try these extra activities:

1 Make a game where a monster has to eat up aliens.

2 To make the game more difficult, program the aliens to move around the screen.

3 Make the car-racing game on pages 22–23 of this book. Take out the **'Touching color'** part of the **'Repeat until'** loop and add an 'if' statement. Now make the score go down by 1 point if the car touches the grass.

4 Try changing the car-racing game so that if the car touches the grass, it moves forward by -1 step. This will make the car slow down.

PAGES 14–15
Starting Python

OBJECTIVES

These pages introduce the Python language. After Logo and Scratch, Python is an excellent next step for children's coding as it uses a more standard text-based approach.

EXTRA HELP

For help installing Python, see page 54 of this book. Make sure children are confident starting up IDLE, the Python editor. Then show them how to set up their screen so that the text editor with their typed code is on the left-hand side. Save and run a simple program. A new window will appear – this shows the output from the program. Show children how to position this on the right-hand side of their screen for ease of working.

```
print("hello")
```

```
>>>
hello
>>>
```

Get children to practise making simple one- or two-line programs until they are happy carrying out these basic tasks. Note that IDLE recognizes commands (such as **print**) and displays them in different colours. This is to help programmers spot mistakes in their code. In our books, we have represented these colours in shades of grey.

PAGES 16–17
Python printing

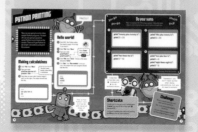

OBJECTIVES

In 'Python printing', children will learn how to use Python to print text on the screen and to make simple calculations. Typing programs in Python requires close attention to detail.

TIP

It is common for children to make small errors when typing in Python code. Unfortunately, the Python editor won't always give helpful feedback if there are mistakes. Here are some tips to avoid problems:

1. Python won't make it obvious when words are typed incorrectly, but if it recognizes a command such as **print** it will change the text to purple.

2. When children are typing in the contents of print brackets – such as **print(123)** – the brackets and 123 will be highlighted if they are typed correctly:

print(123)

Children need to learn to look for these visual clues to know their code is correct.

Python questions

Python loops

OBJECTIVES
Having used selection in Scratch in Book 3 pages 6–13, children will now work with selection in Python. Python's simple approach will help children get a better understanding of selection. Although all the commands have to be typed in, it can be quicker and less fiddly to create a quiz in Python than in Scratch.

TAKING IT FURTHER
Ask children to compare how they would program the same quiz in Python and Scratch. For example:

```
answer=input("What is the capital of England?")
if answer=="London":
    print("Correct")
```

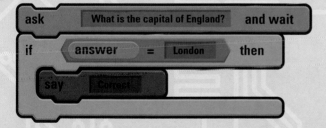

COMMON CONFUSIONS
When using Python, make sure children remember to type the colon (:) and check for the tab after an 'if' command (in these books, we use tabs to indent Python, but many programmers prefer using 4 spaces). Also note that Python is what programmers call 'case-sensitive' – it cares about capital letters when comparing text. It thinks 'London' is not the same as 'london'. In contrast, Scratch is not case-sensitive and treats 'london' as equal to 'London'.

OBJECTIVES
Here we will extend our work on loops by doing some counting in Python. Coding Python loops will reinforce children's understanding of the concept.

TAKING IT FURTHER
1 There is a shortcut to creating Python loops. If you don't care what number the loop starts from, you can just write:

```
for n in range(10):
    print(n)
```

2 If we want the loop to go up in numbers greater than 1, we can use 3 values (or 'arguments') in the brackets. Experiment with this to see how it works:

```
for n in range(0,50,5):
    print(n)
```

EXTRA HELP
One of the main differences between the way Python and Scratch handle loops is that Python also introduces a variable (for example, n) that increases as the loop repeats. This is the case with most modern coding languages. If children need a reminder of variables, remember that we used a variable to keep the score in 'Quiz time' in Book 3 pages 8–9. Compare these Scratch and Python loops:

```
for n in range(0,10):
    print("Hello!")
```

PAGES 22–23
Python graphics

OBJECTIVES

These pages teach children how to create graphics in Python by importing a library of code called 'turtle'. The turtle commands allow children to draw by moving around a turtle or sprite, in a similar manner to the drawing functions in Logo and Scratch. In the 'Loops and graphics' exercises, we will use loops to draw shapes.

TAKING IT FURTHER

By using two loops together, one inside the other, we can create some of the patterns made with Logo in Book 2 pages 8–9. This exercise will reinforce children's understanding of both loops and Python.

In Logo: **repeat 36 [rt 10 repeat 4 [fd 120 rt 90]]**

In Python:

```
from turtle import *
for r in range(0,36):
    rt(10)
    for s in range(0,4):
        fd(120)
        rt(90)
```

We are using **fd** and **rt** instead of forward and right – but either will work in Python. Typing **speed(0)** before any drawing commands will speed things up!

Both programs draw a pattern like this:

PAGES 24–25
Random Python

OBJECTIVES

Here we introduce another library that can be added to Python – this time to create random numbers. Children will learn about the usefulness of randomness in computer games. They will code Python programs to simulate a coin toss and make 'random sandwiches'.

KEY CONCEPT: RANDOM NUMBERS

A good way for children to grasp the concept of randomness is to toss a coin. It is also worthwhile to compare how we program randomness in Python and Scratch. In Python, we import the **random** library. In Scratch, we use commands in the **Operators** group. The commands to pick random numbers are very similar in both languages:

In Python: **randint(1,6)**

In Scratch: **pick random 1 to 6**

Once children have learnt how to use random numbers in Scratch, they can be dropped into any white box that normally has a number in it. For example:
Always drag the **'Pick random'** block from the left end

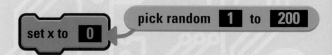

so you can drop it in a number box.

This will make a sprite appear in a random place across the screen.

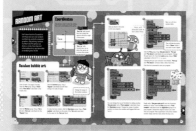

OBJECTIVES

In 'Random art', we return to Scratch to apply what has been learnt about random numbers. We will be making a bubble picture using random coordinates, pen sizes and colours.

OBJECTIVES

These debugging exercises in Scratch and Python will help children to develop the key skills of spotting and fixing mistakes in their coding. In particular, the Python exercises will encourage good proofreading skills, which are essential when working with text-based programming languages.

HOW THE CODE WORKS

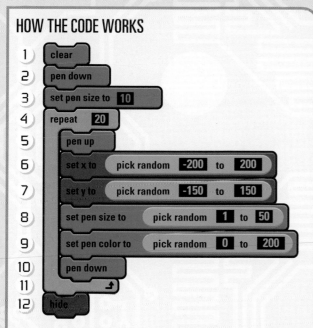

```
1   clear
2   pen down
3   set pen size to 10
4   repeat 20
5       pen up
6       set x to   pick random -200 to 200
7       set y to   pick random -150 to 150
8       set pen size to   pick random 1 to 50
9       set pen color to   pick random 0 to 200
10      pen down
11
12  hide
```

1 Clear the screen.

2 Pen down (so it will draw).

3 Set pen size to 10 pixels.

4 Repeat the commands within the main loop 20 times.

5 Pen up (don't join each dot).

6 Set x (left to right position) to a random number from -200 to 200.

7 Set y (top to bottom position) to a random number from -150 to 150.

8 Set dot size to a random number from 1 to 50 pixels.

9 Choose a random colour.

10 Pen down (draw the dot).

11 Loop back up.

12 Hide the sprite at the end.

EXTRA HELP

Debugging Python code can be a particularly difficult skill to master. Some children will be able to spot the mistakes in exercises 4–7 at first glance. Many children will need a little extra help. Ask them to type the buggy codes into IDLE. Although Python will not correct mistyped words, it will change the colour of commands such as **print** when it recognizes them. When programming anything in Python, remind children to look out for the colour changes and bracket highlighting to check code has been typed correctly.

Random Python graphics

These activities will extend children's learning by combining two Python libraries: random numbers and graphics. By using these libraries with some loops and variables, we can create amazing patterns.

1

RANDOM SQUARE
Start IDLE, the Python editor, and open a new file.

2

Type in the following commands:

```
from turtle import *
from random import *
```

This tells Python to borrow all the commands from the turtle and random libraries and bring them into our program.

3

To start with, we need to move the turtle to a random position on the screen. We can use the **goto** command to do this. It needs two random values: the x position and y position of the square. (For a reminder about x and y coordinates, see page 18 of this book.)

Create a variable called x, with a random value between 0 and 300.

Create a variable called y, with a random value between 0 and 300.

Pen up (don't draw).

Make the turtle go to the point on the screen with coordinates (x,y).

Pen down (start drawing).

This loop draws a square.

```
from turtle import *
from random import *

x=randint(0,300)
y=randint(0,300)
pu()
goto(x,y)
pd()

for s in range(0,4):
    forward(100)
    right(90)
```

Save and run your code to test it. Each time you run it, the square will be drawn in a different place.

DRAWING MULTIPLE RANDOM PATTERNS

We will now extend our program to draw 30 flower patterns on the screen. Each flower pattern will be made of 6 squares rotated around a point. The program will need 3 loops:

- An **inner** loop to draw the square.
- A loop to repeat 6 squares to make the flower pattern.
- An **outer** loop to draw 30 of the flowers, each in a random position.

1 Start IDLE, the Python editor, and open a new file.

2 Type in the following code:

> Import turtle library and random library.

```
from turtle import *
from random import *
```

> Make turtle move quickly.

```
speed(0)
```

> Repeat outer loop 30 times.
> Create a random value for x between -300 and 300.
> Create a random value for y between -300 and 300.
> Pen up (don't draw).
> Move the turtle to (x,y).
> Pen down (start drawing).

```
for p in range(0,30):
    x=randint(-300,300)
    y=randint(-300,300)
    pu()
    goto(x,y)
    pd()
```

> Repeat loop 6 times.
> Turn right 60 degrees.

```
for r in range(0,6):
    right(60)
```

> Now draw each square:
> Repeat inner loop 4 times.
> Move forward 50 pixels.
> Turn right 90 degrees.

```
for s in range(0,4):
    forward(50)
    right(90)
```

3 Save and run your code to test it. It should look rather like this:

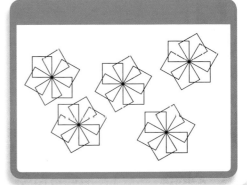

Challenge!

Try adding an extra variable to use as the size of the pattern. Set it to a random value. Use it instead of moving forward 50 in the inner loop.

BOOK 3

Random Python quiz

This project combines many of the key concepts covered so far: inputs, variables and random numbers. We will also be using different types of variables. We will create a quiz asking 10 random times tables questions, and also counting the total answered correctly.

ASKING A RANDOM QUESTION

Before making a quiz with 10 questions, we will try making a quiz with 1 question.

1. First we need to create two random numbers for our question — let's call them **a** and **b**.

2. Next we need to ask the player what **a** times **b** is.

3. Finally we need to check if the player is correct or not, then tell them.

1

Start IDLE, the Python editor, and open a new file.

2

Type in the following commands:

Import random library.

Create a variable called **a** with a random value between 1 and 12. Create a variable called **b** with a random value between 1 and 12.

Ask the question, for example: 'What is 5 times 4?'

Wait for the player to answer and store it in a variable called **answer**.

The answer will be a 'string'. We will convert it to an integer so we can compare it to **a times b**.

Check to see if the answer is equal to **a times b**. If equal, display **correct**. Else display **wrong**.

```python
from random import *

a=randint(1,12)
b=randint(1,12)

print("What is",a,"times",b)

answer=input("?")

answer=int(answer)

if answer==a*b:
    print("correct")
else:
    print("wrong")
```

IDLE will keep adding tabs after you type **if**. You need to delete one of these before typing **else**.

STRINGS AND INTEGERS

We use variables to store information. Some information, such as the score in a game, will be a number. If it is a whole number, we call that an integer. Other information, such as your name, will be made up of letters. Information that is made up of letters is called a string. A variable created by an input statement will be a string, even if it has numbers in it. Python treats strings and integers in different ways. It thinks 20 is not the same as "20". If we need to compare the value of a string to an integer, first we need to convert the string into an integer. To make that conversion, we used **answer=int(answer)** in our quiz.

ADDING MORE QUESTIONS AND A SCORE

To make our quiz ask 10 questions, we need to create an outer loop than fits around the main part of our code. We also need to add a score variable that will be set to zero at the start, and will go up if a player answers a question correctly. Finally, we need to show the score at the end of the game.

1 Start a new file, or edit your current file.

2 Type in the following code:

Set score variable (s) to zero.

Start a loop that runs from 1 to 10.

Ask the question – for example: 'Question 3 What is 3 times 8?'

If the answer is correct, add 1 to the score (s).

Display the number of correct answers (s).

```python
from random import *

s=0
for q in range(1,11):

    a=randint(1,12)
    b=randint(1,12)

    print("Question",q,"What is",a,"times",b)

    answer=input("?")
    answer=int(answer)

    if answer==a*b:
        print("correct")
        s=s+1
    else:
        print("wrong")

print("You scored",s,"out of 10")
```

```
>>>
Question 1 What is 4 times 7
?28
correct
```

Make sure that your code is indented like above. Use the 'Tab' or 'Delete' keys to make it match if you need to. Without the correct indents, your code won't work!

PAGES 6–7
Creating web pages

OBJECTIVES

These pages will get young coders started with producing their own web pages. Children will learn how web pages use special **<tags>** to mark different parts of the page. Like most professional programmers, we will start by creating pages on our computer and testing them 'locally', rather than working online with 'live' web pages. Children will learn how to create a page in a text editor, save it as .html and open it in a web browser – a process that needs mastering before we move forward.

EXTRA HELP

Children will benefit from getting the hang of file saving and handling before moving on to more complex HTML and JavaScript coding. Here are some practice tips:

1. Practise using the text editor. Make sure children can find the text editor themselves. If children are using a Mac, first they need to click the **'TextEdit'** menu then **'Preferences'**. Choose **'Plain text'** and uncheck **'Smart quotes'**.

2. Children need to work on their file handling. Make sure they know how to save files, and how to find them once they have been saved. It is worth creating a folder on the desktop (or documents area) that they can access easily and keep all their work in.

3. Make sure children understand that web pages must be saved as .html files or they won't work properly.

PAGES 8–9
Using HTML

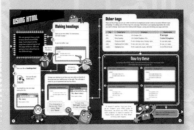

OBJECTIVES

Once children have become familiar with creating a simple 3-line web page, saving it and opening it in a browser, they will be ready to look at using different tags. The first tags they will have encountered are **<html>** and **</html>** at the start and end of a document. Now we introduce paragraph and heading tags. Children will also learn how to emphasize parts of their text with tags such as **<em>**.

TAKING IT FURTHER

For extra tag practice, start a new HTML document in your text editor. Add **<html>** and **</html>** tags to the page. Write a list of animals between them. Save and test the page. Now edit the page, using heading tags to make different animals larger and smaller. For example:

Text editor – animals.html

```
<html>
  <h1>Elephant</h1>
  <h5>Mouse</h5>
  <h2>Tiger</h2>
  <h6>Fly</h6>
</html>
```

Browser

 //desktop/animals.html

Elephant
Mouse

Tiger
Fly

OBJECTIVES

These pages start by teaching children more about URLs (web addresses). We then move on to the key skill of creating hyperlinks to other web pages. Children will become familiar with the anchor tag: `<a>`.

EXTRA HELP

Some text editors will use 'smart quotes' and change vertical quotes (') for angled ones ('). If this happens, refer to 'Extra help' on the opposite page to switch off this feature, or consider using a dedicated text editor – see 'Tip' on the right.

TAKING IT FURTHER

Ask children to make a list of international country codes used in URLs, starting with co.uk. This part of the domain is called the 'suffix'. Can children discover any suffixes that reveal that a website is run by a charity, government or educational organization?

OBJECTIVES

Now children are familiar with how to create links, they will create a page of their favourite links. They will use their own anchor tags (`<a>` and `</a>`), combining them with some of the heading and paragraph tags already learnt.

COMMON CONFUSIONS

Some children may get mixed up about what goes inside the different parts of the anchor tags on a web page – `<a>` and `</a>`. Make sure they understand that the `<a href = >` part needs to contain the URL, while the part between the anchor tags will be shown on the web page as the text to click to link to the URL. Children also need to remember to put quotes around the URL.

TIP

A basic text editor, such as Notepad or TextEdit, will allow children to start creating web pages. It will also encourage them to look in detail at how a page is built. Once they get beyond simple experimenting, it is worth downloading a dedicated, more advanced HTML editor. There are many available for free: see page 56 for more information on downloading one.

A good HTML editor will require children to learn how to code and not do it all for them, but will provide features to support them, such as:

- Auto-colouring text to emphasize tags, keywords, strings and numbers.
- Auto-completing code to save time.
- Indicating that tags, brackets and quotes have been closed and have matching pairs.
- Allowing children to have multiple files open at the same time to work on.

PAGES 14–15
Colour it!

PAGES 16–17
Adding JavaScript

OBJECTIVES

'Colour it!' will teach children how to change the colour and style of objects on a web page. Large websites do this with additional files containing CSS (Cascading Style Sheets; see page 58). Here we use a simpler approach to explore the concept, by putting style attributes inside tags.

TAKING IT FURTHER

Children could also learn how to change the font their text is printed in:

1. Start a new HTML file in your text editor.

2. Type in this code:
```
<html>
 <h1>Fruit</h1>
 <p>Apples</p>
</html>
```

3. Save and test your page.

4. Edit the second line to add a style attribute **<h1 style="font-family:Arial">** (the way you have done previously to change colour). This will change the font family (font name) of the text.

5. Experiment with other fonts. Try using Impact and Tahoma first.

If you set a font family that has more than one word in its name, you need to put quotes round it. These need to be different quotes from the ones you used to set the style attribute! For example, here single quotes are used around the font name, double quotes around the style attribute:

<h1 style="font-family:'Comic Sans MS'">

OBJECTIVES

So far children have been coding their web pages only with HTML. To make their web pages more interactive, now they will learn how to combine their HTML coding with another language, JavaScript. They will learn how to add a 'listener' to make some JavaScript run when a button is clicked.

TAKING IT FURTHER

Once children have mastered the exercises in Book 4 pages 16–17, they could create a new web page with three buttons. Each button needs to have a riddle written on it. Add onclick listeners to each button so that when the button is clicked, the answer is shown as a message. For example, try using this code (type it all on one line):

<button onclick='alert("A bee flying backwards")'>What goes zzub zzub? </button>

JavaScript loops

OBJECTIVES

Now we will do some sums and counting, using JavaScript loops and variables. Children will probably have used loops and variables before – whether making patterns or keeping scores in Logo or Scratch (see Book 2), or counting in Python (see Book 3). In this book, turn to page 16 for a refresher on loops, and page 20 for a reminder on variables.

TAKING IT FURTHER

In the counting exercises in Book 4 page 19, the numbers displayed by a loop are shown next to each other. We can force the web browser to show each on a separate line by telling it to show pre-formatted text, using a **<pre>** tag:

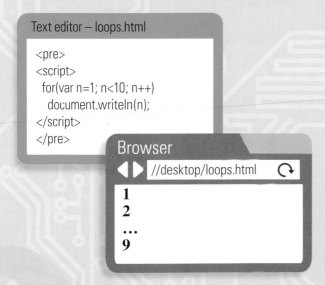

Text editor – loops.html

```
<pre>
<script>
 for(var n=1; n<10; n++)
   document.writeln(n);
</script>
</pre>
```

Browser

//desktop/loops.html

```
1
2
…
9
```

To make a JavaScript loop count up in 5s, change the right-hand side of the loop from **n++** to **n+=5**.
For example, to write the numbers 0, 5, 10, 15, 20, use: **for(var n=0; n<21; n+=5)**. Now try these exercises (answers are on page 62):

1 Make a loop that shows 0, 10, 20, 30, 40.

2 Make a loop that shows 2, 4, 6, 8, 10.

JavaScript functions

OBJECTIVES

These pages introduce the idea of functions. Functions are a sequence of commands that perform a specific task every time that function is 'called' (run). The idea is explained through the analogy of writing an instruction that tells a robot to make a sandwich. The instructions work whatever sandwich fillings the robot is using. The idea is then put into practice by creating a function that will ask a question and check the answer is correct. Children will use this function to code a quiz.

KEY CONCEPT: FUNCTIONS

Functions are an important concept in coding. Here are some reasons to create and use your own functions:

1 Using a function means that you don't have to repeat lines of code – we just 'call' the function whenever it is needed rather than repeating the same commands over and over.

2 Functions make long programs easier to read.

3 Functions make programs more flexible – a function can be used in more than one situation.

4 It is much easier to add a 'call' to a JavaScript function into an HTML listener than write multiple lines of code.

PAGES 22–23
JS functions with HTML

OBJECTIVES

These pages continue our work on JavaScript functions. This time we will be combining JavaScript and HTML coding. The activities here show children how to create a function that changes the background colour of a web page.

TAKING IT FURTHER

To try something extra, we can create a similar function to change the colour of text on a web page.

1. Start a new web page in your text editor. Type in the following:

Text editor – creepyhouse.html

```
<html>
<h1>The Creepy House</h1>
<p>Once upon a time</p>
<button onclick="setcol('red')">Red</button>
<button onclick="setcol('blue')">Blue</button>
<script>
  function setcol(col){
     document.body.style.color=col;
  }
</script>
</html>
```

This program is very similar to the one in Book 4 page 23, but it changes the colour of the text instead of the background colour. It uses **style.color** to change the text colour.

2. Save and test your file in the same way as on page 23.

3. Add more buttons and colours – have fun experimenting!

PAGES 24–25
Pets project

OBJECTIVES

This project will teach children to create a simple website by linking together several pages of information. They will also learn how to add images to their web pages. As long as their website will not be online, children can use whatever images they like – but if the website will be for public display, they need to be aware of copyright and e-safety (see Book 4 pages 26–27). Children should always be closely supervised when downloading images from the internet.

TAKING IT FURTHER

Creating small projects with multiple pages can give children very good practice at handling files and creating links. You can help them by creating a separate folder for each project. Here are some ideas for extra website projects:

1. This term's history topic, such as an ancient civilization and its artefacts.

2. Your favourite sports and sports stars.

3. Reviews of your favourite books or films.

4. Science topics, such as materials and their uses.

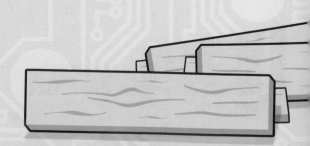

Sharing your website

Debugging

OBJECTIVES

These pages explain how children can upload websites they have created. Children can develop their coding and HTML skills while staying offline (without uploading), but sometimes they may enjoy getting an audience for their work. Make sure children are closely supervised if they are putting any information online. Please follow the e-safety guidelines below, together with any other rules you have at home or school about internet use.

OBJECTIVES

In these exercises, children will need to fix some example pieces of HTML and JavaScript code with bugs in. The pieces of code feature all the key concepts we have learnt in Book 4: links, styling, loops and functions.

E-SAFETY GUIDELINES

If you are working with a group of children, it is worth displaying these guidelines where everyone can read them and keep them in mind:

1 Don't share personal information online – such as your full name, address or email address.

2 Don't include photos of you or your family.

3 Don't write anything unkind about other people on your site.

TIP

Children could try using the console, a debugging tool built into most web browsers. It will help them to see that there are errors and where they are, although the messages may appear quite technical at first.

Showing the console:

On a Mac, using Chrome:

alt + cmd + i

On a PC, using Internet Explorer or Chrome:

F12

Browser

//desktop/mypage html

My page

The console will appear here or at the bottom of your browser.

Typical messages in the console:

'scor' is not defined - mypage.html:3
Means the browser doesn't know the variable or function called **scor**. This message may show up when a variable or function is spelt incorrectly. The error is probably in line 3.

Unexpected token ILLEGAL - mypage.html:7
or
Unterminated string constant - mypage.html:7
Means there is a quote or double quote missing somewhere in line 7 – for example, **alert('hello)**.

Countries website

This project will extend children's use of HTML by creating a mini website with a number of new techniques. They will learn how to use an image as a link and how to change the size of an image. These are very useful skills to apply to other projects.

1

Start a new web page in your text editor and type in the following text:

Text editor

```
<html>
  <h1>Countries</h1>
</html>
```

2

Make a new folder for your project called **'Countries'**. Save your file there and call it **index.html**.

To make a new folder on a Mac, click **'New folder'** after clicking **'File'** and **'Save'**. On a PC, right-click in the save box then click **'New'** and **'Folder'**.

3

Open the **Countries** folder and double-click the **index.html** file to test it.

4

Arrange your desktop so you have the Countries folder, your text editor and your browser all visible at once.

Double-click the Countries folder to open it. You will keep all the files for your website in here.

Files: desktop/Countries

index.html   paris.jpg

Text editor – index.html

```
<html>
  <h1>Countries</h1>
</html>
```

Browser
//desktop/Countries/index.html

Countries

You need photos of Paris and Rome (or somewhere else if you prefer!). Ask an adult to help you search for some online. Drag the photos into your Countries folder and name them **paris.jpg** and **rome.jpg**.

Always ask an adult if you can search for photos on the web.

5

Click **'File'** and **'New'** to start the next page. Type in this code:

```html
<html>
 <h1>France</h1>
 <img src ="paris.jpg">
</html>
```

Save this page as **france.html** in the Countries folder.

6

Edit your **index.html** file:

Start of anchor link

Picture within link

Text within link

End of anchor link

Text editor – index.html

```html
<html>
 <h1>Countries</h1>
 <a href="france.html">
  <img src ="paris.jpg">
  France
 </a>
</html>
```

Save the file!

7

Refresh the page.
Click the 'France' link and the France page will load in your browser.

Browser
//desktop/Countries/index.html

Countries

France

Browser
//desktop/Countries/france.html

France

8

Both pictures will be quite large. The one on the France page can be left that size, but on the Index page we need to make it smaller. (For an online website, you would also need to make the photo small to make it quicker to download.) Edit the 4th line of code in your **index.html** file:

<img src ="paris.jpg" width="100" >

Set the width to **100**. This means 100 pixels.

Save the file and refresh the page to test it. The photo's height should also have changed automatically.

9

Now add another page for Italy and save it (see step 5 for how). You will also need to make another link for it in your index file, so edit your **index.html** file like this:

Use **
** to make a line break to start a new line.

Text editor – index.html

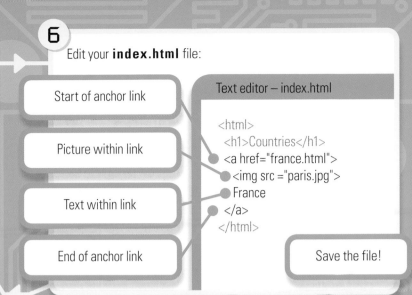

```html
<html>
 <h1>Countries</h1>
 <a href="france.html">
  <img src ="paris.jpg" width="100">
  France
 </a>
 <br>
 <a href="italy.html">
  <img src ="rome.jpg" width="100">
  Italy
 </a>
</html>
```

10

Add more information about each country on its page. Use **<p>** paragraph **</p>** tags around the information. Look back at Book 4 page 14 to change the colour of pages and text.

Embedding

This activity looks at how children can add extra resources to their web pages such as videos and maps. They will learn how to include these objects within a new HTML object called an iframe, and how to set the size for the embedded (added) object.

EMBEDDING A VIDEO

There are times when you want to add a video to a web page. If you own the video and it is stored on your computer or server, you could include it like we added the photos in the previous project. Alternatively you could make a link to it if it is on another site. Embedding is something inbetween the two – it looks as if the video is on your website, but really it is being shown from another site.

1 With an adult's help, find a video online that you want to embed.

Always ask an adult if you can search for videos on the web.

2 Look on the web page to find a **'Share'** button, then click it.

3 Click the **'Embed'** button. Highlight all the code. Right-click your mouse and choose **'Copy'**.

Share	**Embed**	**Email**	✕

`<iframe width="560" height="315" src="https://www...  ></iframe>`

On a Mac, you'll have to hold the **'Control'** key when you click.

4 Start a new HTML file in your text editor. Type in a basic HTML file:

Right-click your mouse here, and choose 'Paste'.

The iframe code should appear in your HTML file. If it doesn't, go back to the video and do step 3 again.

Save and test the file in your browser.

Text editor – video.html

```
<html>
 <h1>Videos</h1>
 <p>Here is a video about London</p>
  <iframe width="560" height="315" src...
</html>
```

Browser

//desktop/video.html

Videos
Here is a video about London

Embedding a map

We can embed a map in a similar way.

1

Find an online map you want to embed. Zoom in to the level you want.

2

Find the **'Share'** button and click it. (On Google Maps, click the cog ✿ first.)

3

Click the **'Embed'** button. Highlight all the code, right-click your mouse and choose **'Copy'**.

Embed Map ✕

`<iframe src="https://www.google.com/maps/embed...</iframe>`

On a Mac, you'll have to hold the **'Control'** key when you click.

4

Start a new HTML file in your text editor. Type in a basic HTML file:

> Right-click your mouse here, and choose **'Paste'**.

The iframe code should appear in your HTML file. If it doesn't, go back to the video and do step 3 again.

Save and test the file in your browser.

Text editor – map.html

```
<html>
 <h1>London</h1>
 <p>Here is a map of central London</p>
  <iframe src="https://www.google.com/maps...
</html>
```

Browser

◀▶ //desktop/map.html ↻

London
Here is a map of central London

CHANGING THE IFRAME SIZE

Look through the iframe code that you have pasted in. There should be two 'attributes' called **width** and **height**. These attributes tell the web page how big the iframe should be. If you carefully change these values, you can make the iframe (and the map or video it embeds) bigger or smaller.

`<iframe width="560" height="315" src="https://www...  ></iframe>`

> Change the value between the quotes.

Functions in Scratch

In Book 4, we learnt how to create JavaScript functions. To expand children's understanding of the vital concept of functions, it is useful to teach them how to create functions in other languages – here we will look at Scratch. This activity also serves as a simple introduction to the concept of functions. For help with using Scratch, turn to page 52.

DRAW A SIMPLE SQUARE
Before we create a function to draw a square, we will draw a square using a loop.

1 Start Scratch. Click on the **Control** group of commands.

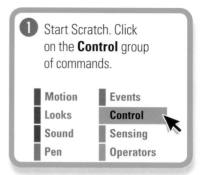

2 Drag a **'Repeat'** block onto the scripts area.

3 Change the number of loops to repeat to 4.

4 Click on the **Motion** group.

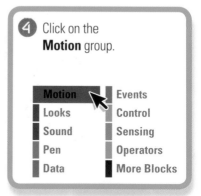

5 Drag in a **'Move steps'** block and a **'Turn'** block, then change the amount to turn to 90 degrees.

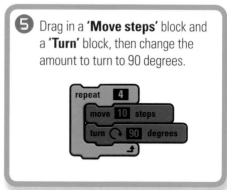

6 Drag a **'Pen down'** block from the Pen group.

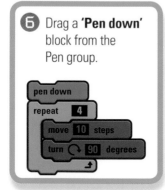

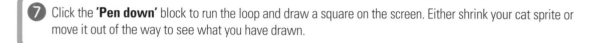

7 Click the **'Pen down'** block to run the loop and draw a square on the screen. Either shrink your cat sprite or move it out of the way to see what you have drawn.

WHY USE A FUNCTION?
The code above works fine, but every time we want to draw a square we need to use 4 lines of code. We also need extra code if we want to change the size of the square.

We are now going to learn how to make a function called **square**, which will do the job in one word. We are going to pass the square function a number to say how big it will be.

Create a square function

1
Click on the **More blocks** group.

Pen	Operators
Data	**More Blocks**

2
Click **'Make a block'**.

Make a Block

3
Type 'square' as a name for your function.

square

4
Don't click 'OK' yet. First click **Options** and **'Add number input'**.

▼ Options

Add number input:

5
Your block should look like this:

square   number1

Click **'OK'**.

OK

6
Start adding in code to draw a square (see opposite page).

define   square   number1
pen down
repeat   4

7
Complete the code:

define   square   number1
pen down
repeat   4
    move   10   steps
    turn ↻   90   degrees

8
Drag the **'Number1'** box down to the **'Move steps'** box.

define   square   number1
pen down
repeat   4
    move   number1   steps
    turn ↻   90   degrees

This will allow you to choose the size of the square and pass it to the function.

USE THE SQUARE FUNCTION

Now we can use our square function to draw patterns. For each pattern, we will pass our square function some numbers to tell it how big the squares will be.

Click on the **More blocks** group. Drag the **'Square'** code block onto the scripts area. Now try creating these 3 programs on the scripts area. Click on each of these programs in turn to see what they draw. Turn to page 62 for the answers.

1
square   50
square   100
square   150

2
square   50
turn ↻   15   degrees
square   50
turn ↻   15   degrees
square   50
turn ↻   15   degrees

3
repeat   24
    square   100
    turn ↻   15   degrees

Functions in Python

These activities can be used as an extension to the work on Scratch functions that we did on the previous pages. You might also use them as a stand-alone lesson in functions to extend children's understanding of Python. For help using Python, turn to page 54.

1

DRAW A SIMPLE SQUARE
Start IDLE, the Python editor.

2

Click **'File'** and **'New'** then type in:

```
from turtle import *
for n in range(0,4):
    forward(200)
    right(90)
```

Save the program as **shapes.py**.

For more ideas about using Python, see Book 3.

3

Click **'Run'** then **'Run module'** to test the program.

A new window will open to show the turtle graphics:

Create a square function

1

Start a new file and type in the following program:

This line starts defining the function.

The function uses similar code to before but, instead of using 200 as the amount to move forward, it uses a variable called s.

```
from turtle import *

def square(s):
    for n in range(0,4):
        forward(s)
        right(90)

square(100)
```

This line 'calls' the function and passes it a value (100) to use as the side length of the square.

2

Save the program as **squares.py**.

3

Click **'Run'** then **'Run module'** to test the program.

A new window will open to show the turtle graphics:

USE THE SQUARE FUNCTION

Now edit the last part of your code to try these programs. Save and run them to test them out. What do they draw? Check the answers on page 62.

1

```
from turtle import *

def square(s):
    for n in range(0,4):
        forward(s)
        right(90)

square(50)
square(100)
square(150)
```

2

```
from turtle import *

def square(s):
    for n in range(0,4):
        forward(s)
        right(90)

square(100)
right(15)
square(100)
right(15)
square(100)
right(15)
```

3

```
from turtle import *

def square(s):
    for n in range(0,4):
        forward(s)
        right(90)

for r in range(0,24):
    square(50)
    right(15)
```

4

```
from turtle import *

def square(s):
    for n in range(0,4):
        forward(s)
        right(90)

left(90)
forward(100)
for r in range(0,10):
    square(40)
    right(36)
```

5

```
from turtle import *

def square(s):
    for n in range(0,4):
        forward(s)
        right(90)

for r in range(0,36):
    square(50)
    right(10)
```

With Python we need to be careful to use 'Tab' to indent the lines properly.

Challenge!

Now experiment with drawing your own patterns using the square function.

The simple programming language Logo is an excellent tool for children to learn some simple coding. Each instruction they type will have an immediate effect, enabling them to quickly explore and experiment. With a small number of short commands, they can create simple drawings, shapes and patterns.

GETTING HOLD OF LOGO

Because Logo was designed over 40 years ago, it won't allow you to create the same sort of games as some other computer coding languages, but it is a great way to learn about some key coding concepts.

If you are using a PC, it is worth downloading Logo. The online versions use the same instructions but can be a bit more fiddly to use. You can download a version for free from:
www.softronix.com/logo.html

Alternatively, both Mac and PC users can work with Logo online. Visit:
www.calormen.com/jslogo/
or
http://turtleacademy.com/playground/en

USING LOGO

To get started with Logo, just click in the command box and type a command (see opposite for useful commands). For example, type **fd 50** and press **'Enter'**. Each version of Logo is slightly different. Some have **'Run'** buttons and some don't. If your version doesn't, press **'Enter'** after typing a command.

There are two ways to type longer programs that have multiple commands. Children can type the first command, then press 'Enter', then the second command, press 'Enter' and so on. Alternatively, to type all the commands in one go, type the first command, then press 'Space', type the second command, press 'Space' and so on.
For example: **fd 50 rt 90 fd 50 lt 90 fd 100 – then press 'Enter'**.

Press the up and down cursor keys to bring back the last few commands you have typed.

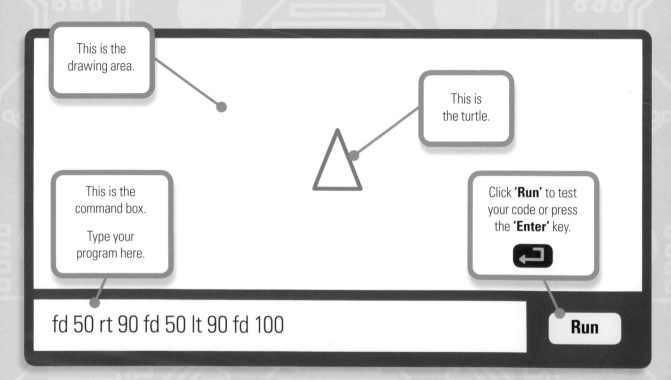

This is the drawing area.

This is the turtle.

This is the command box.

Type your program here.

Click **'Run'** to test your code or press the **'Enter'** key.

fd 50 rt 90 fd 50 lt 90 fd 100

Run

USEFUL LOGO COMMANDS

DIRECTING THE TURTLE

fd 50	Move forward 50 steps.
rt 90	Turn right 90 degrees.
lt 90	Turn left 90 degrees.
bk 50	Move backward 50 steps.
cs	Clear the drawing box.
seth 0	Make the turtle point up.
st	Show turtle.
ht	Hide turtle.

You can type 'forward' instead of 'fd'. It doesn't matter in Logo if you use capital letters or not. Most other languages are more fussy. Remember you can change the number after the command, to alter how far the turtle turns or moves. This number is called the parameter.

POSITIONING THE TURTLE

setpos[100 200]	Set the position of the turtle to 100, 200.
setx 100	Set the x coordinate (left to right) to 100.
sety 200	Set the y coordinate (bottom to top) to 200.
wrap	When the turtle goes off the edge of the screen, wrap around and re-appear on the other side.
fence	When the turtle reaches the edge of the screen, hit an invisible fence and stop.

DRAWING

pu	Pen up: lift the pen up and stop drawing.
pd	Pen down: put the pen down to draw.
setpc 5	Set the pen to colour number 5. (Most computer languages use numbers to represent colours.)
setpensize 5	Set thickness of line drawn by turtle to 5.

LOOPS

repeat	Repeat a sequence of commands a specific number of times. For example: **repeat 4 [fd 100 rt 90]** will repeat four times, forward 100 then right 90 degrees. Both square brackets must be included to make the code work.

PRINTING

print 10+10	Output 20 on the screen.
print heading	Print the heading (angle the turtle is facing) on the screen.
print xcor	Print the current x value of the turtle on the screen.
print ycor	Print the current y value of the turtle on the screen.
ct	Clear any printed text from the screen.

ANGLES

Learners need a basic understanding of degrees to make use of Logo. Knowing that 90 degrees make a right angle or quarter-turn is necessary to draw simple shapes. However, Logo also gives children a perfect environment to explore and develop the concept of angles. Once your children have grasped how to draw a square using **rt 90** to turn the corners, ask them to try changing the 90 to 45 and see what happens.

ESTIMATION

Once children have learnt how to move the turtle 10 or 20 steps forward, try asking them questions like: 'How many steps will we need to move forward to reach the edge of the screen?' Or put your finger on the screen and ask: 'How many steps will move the turtle to my finger?"

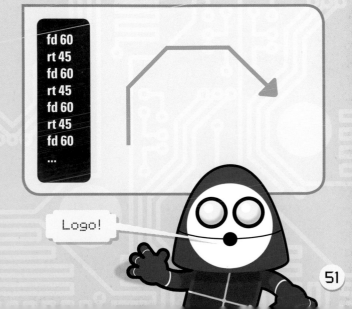

```
fd 60
rt 45
fd 60
rt 45
fd 60
rt 45
fd 60
...
```

Logo!

Scratch is a programming language that uses a similar approach to Logo, making a turtle (called a 'sprite' in Scratch) move around the screen. However, with Scratch you drag and join commands instead of typing them. Scratch is great fun for learning to code games and creating graphics and sound effects.

GETTING HOLD OF SCRATCH

You can use Scratch on a PC or Mac by opening your web browser and going to:
http://scratch.mit.edu
Then click **'Try it out'** or **'Create'**.

There is a very similar website called 'Snap', which also works on iPads. It is available here:
http://snap.berkeley.edu/run

If you want to run Scratch without using the internet, you can download it from here:
http://scratch.mit.edu/scratch2download/

USING SCRATCH

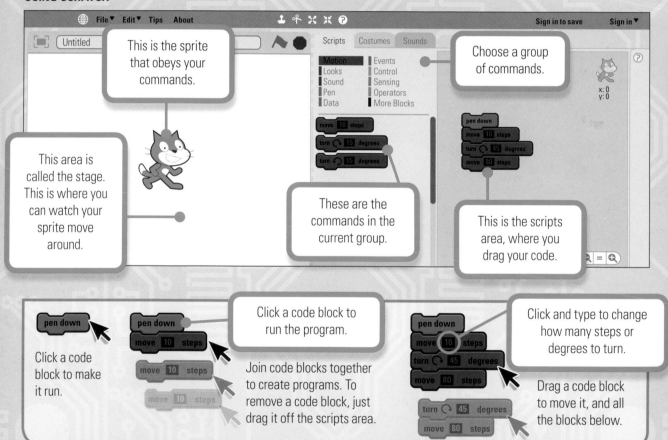

This is the sprite that obeys your commands.

Choose a group of commands.

This area is called the stage. This is where you can watch your sprite move around.

These are the commands in the current group.

This is the scripts area, where you drag your code.

Click a code block to run the program.

Click a code block to make it run.

Join code blocks together to create programs. To remove a code block, just drag it off the scripts area.

Click and type to change how many steps or degrees to turn.

Drag a code block to move it, and all the blocks below.

SAVING YOUR WORK

Click the **'File'** menu at the top of the page on the left. Then click:

Download to your computer – to save a file.
Upload from your computer – to open a file you saved earlier.
New – to start some new work.

USEFUL SCRATCH COMMANDS

MOTION GROUP

`move 10 steps` — Move sprite forward.

`turn ↻ 15 degrees` — Rotate sprite right.

`turn ↺ 15 degrees` — Rotate sprite left.

`point in direction 90 ▼` — Point the sprite up, down, left or right.

`point towards ▼` `mouse-pointer` — Point the sprite towards the mouse or another sprite.

`set x to 0` — Set sprite x coordinate (left to right).

`set y to 0` — Set sprite y coordinate (up or down).

SOUND GROUP

`play sound` `meow` `meow` `record` — Play or record a sound file.

`play note 60 ▼ for 0.5 beats` — Play a musical note.

`set instrument to 1 ▼` — Choose which instrument will play it.

`play drum 1 ▼ for 0.25 beats` — Play a drum beat.

EVENTS GROUP

`when ⚑ clicked` — Run commands below when the green flag is clicked.

`when space ▼ key pressed` — Run commands below when the selected key is pressed.

SENSING GROUP

`ask what's your name? ▼ and wait` — Ask the user a question.

`answer` — Stores the answer to a question.

`touching ▼ ?` — Use with 'Repeat until' or 'if' to check whether objects are touching.

`touching color ?` — Use with 'Repeat until' or 'if' to check the colour the sprite is touching.

LOOKS GROUP

`say Hello!` — Show message.

`say Hello! for 2 secs` — Show message then hide it.

`show` — Show sprite.

`hide` — Hide sprite (make it disappear).

PEN GROUP

`clear` — Clear the screen.

`pen down` — Draw when the sprite moves.

`pen up` — Don't draw.

`set pen color to 1` — Choose colour to draw with.

`set pen size to 1` — Choose line thickness.

CONTROL GROUP

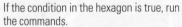

`repeat 10` — Repeat commands inside the 'C' 10 times.

`forever` — Repeat commands inside the 'C' forever.

`repeat until` — Repeat commands until the condition in the hexagon is true.

`if then` — If the condition in the hexagon is true, run the commands.

`if then else` — If the condition in the hexagon is true, run the commands in the top 'C', else run the commands in the bottom 'C'.

OPERATORS GROUP

`= ` — Use with 'Repeat until' or 'if' to check values are equal.

`pick random 1 to 10` — Make a random number.

COMMON PROBLEMS

1. Commands are in the wrong order. Try swapping blocks around to see if that fixes the problem.

2. Children often confuse turning left with turning right, or setting x with setting y coordinates. Keep handy a diagram or a 'paper turtle' marked with L and R.

3. When more than one sprite is used, it is easy to forget to click on the correct sprite before adding or changing code.

4. Some settings persist. For example, try clicking 'Pen down' before making a program to draw a shape (but omitting the 'Pen down' command from within the program), then save the program. The shape will draw because Scratch 'remembers' the 'Pen down' command. However, if you open the program the next day, the shape won't be drawn, because 'Pen down' was not part of the program.

5. The 'Touching color' command block is tricky to use. Make sure the colour being checked for is exactly the same as the required colour by using the colour picker.

Python is a computer language that will help children learn more complex ideas and techniques. With Python, all commands need to be typed carefully to create programs. Python is free to download and comes with something called IDLE that lets you type and edit Python programs.

GETTING HOLD OF PYTHON

Installing and running Python on a PC:
1. Go to **www.python.org**.
2. Click **'Downloads'** then choose **'Download Python'** (version 3.4 or higher).
3. Double-click the downloaded file, then follow the instructions on screen.
4. Click the **'Start'** button, click **'Python'** then click **'IDLE'**. (In Windows 8, go to the top right of the screen and click **'Search'**, then type in 'idle' and click the program to run it.)

Installing and running Python on a Mac:
1. Go to **www.python.org**.
2. Click **'Downloads'** then choose **'Download Python'** (version 3.4 or higher).
3. Double-click the downloaded file, then follow the instructions on screen.
4. To start using Python quickly, click **'Spotlight'**.
5. Type 'idle' then press **'Enter'**.

USING PYTHON
When you want to create a new Python program:

- Start **IDLE**, the Python editor.

- Click **'File'** then **'New'**. Type your code into the IDLE window.

- Before you run a program, you first need to save it (see right).

- Then click the **'Run'** menu and **'Run module'** to run it, or press **'F5'**. This will open a new window to show the output from your program. If you are using the turtle library, another window will open to show the graphics output from your code.

SAVING YOUR WORK
Click the **'File'** menu at the top of the page on the left. Then click:

Save – To save a file onto your computer.

Open – To open a file you have saved earlier. Or click **'File'** and **'Recent files'** then choose your file.

New – To start some new work.

MAKING AN ICON FOR PYTHON ON A MAC
This will make Python easier to find on a Mac:

1. Open **'Finder'**.
2. Click on **'Applications'**.
3. Click on **'Python'**.
4. Drag the **IDLE** icon to the **'dock'** (menu bar) at the bottom or side of the screen.

USEFUL PYTHON COMMANDS, LIBRARIES AND FUNCTIONS

COMMAND	WHAT IT DOES	EXAMPLE
print	Print a string on the screen.	print("Hello")
input	Ask the user to enter a value.	n=input("How old are you?")
if	Test if a condition is true or not.	if n==10:
else	Run a block of code following an 'if' statement, when the condition is false.	else: ....print("wrong")
for...in...range	Make a repeating loop.	for n in range(0,10):
from...import...	Import a code library, for example containing graphics commands.	from random import *
turtle	A graphics library.	from turtle import *
forward or fd	Move the turtle forward.	forward(10)
left or lt	Rotate the turtle left.	left(90)
right or rt	Rotate the turtle right.	right(45)
pendown or pd	Pen down: draw when the turtle moves.	pd()
penup or pu	Pen up: don't draw when the turtle moves.	penup()
goto	Move the turtle to specific coordinates.	goto(200,100)
color	Set the colour for the turtle to draw with. Note the American spelling: 'color'.	color("orange")
random	A library to create and work with random numbers.	from random import *
randint	Create a random number between two values.	dice=randint(1,6)
choice	Randomly select an item from a list.	days=["M","Tu","W","Th","F"] print(choice(days))
int	Convert a string of characters to an integer.	n=int("10")
tab	The 'Tab' key can be used to indent code after an 'if' statement (Python also accepts 4 spaces).	....print("You are ten.")

COMMON PROBLEMS

1 Brackets and quotes are missing or not matching. Encourage children to check their typing. Python will give some warnings: **"EOL while scanning string literal"** means there is a missing quote; **"unexpected EOF while parsing"** means something is missing at the end of the line, often a bracket.

2 Indents are incorrect. Don't forget to use tabs after 'if' commands and for loops. IDLE adds these automatically, but if children want several things to happen after an 'if' statement they may need to add tabs. If they only want one thing to happen, they will need to delete a tab.

3 The range in a 'for' loop is incorrect. The range starts with the 1st number, but stops before the 2nd number. For example, **for n in range(1,10)** makes a loop run from 1 to 9. Making a random number is different: **randint(1,10)** creates random numbers from 1 to 10.

4 Accidentally deleting saved work by choosing **'Save'** instead of **'Open'** when trying to retrieve a program: this will replace a previous file with a blank one! Children should retrieve their work from the **'Recent files'** list.

5 Code is mistyped. Encourage children to wait for IDLE to automatically colour and highlight their code as they type.

TECHNICAL GUIDE

There are many different ways of creating web pages. This series focusses on giving children an introduction to **HTML** (Hyper Text Mark-up Language), the language of the web. A program called a text editor (Notepad on a PC, and TextEdit on a Mac) is needed to start writing HTML. You will need a browser (such as Internet Explorer, Safari or Chrome) to view it.

USING A TEXT EDITOR

On a PC:

Click: **'Start'**, **'Programs'**, **'Accessories'** then **'Notepad'**

For Windows 8: At top right of the screen, click **'Search'**, type **'Notepad'**, then click the program to run it.

On a Mac:

Click: **'Spotlight'**
Type: **'textedit'**
Press: **'Enter'**

At top right of the screen

If you are using TextEdit on a Mac:
You need to make sure the page is being saved in the right way and that smart quotes are turned off. Click on the **'TextEdit'** menu and **'Preferences'**. Then click **'Plain text'** and uncheck **'Smart quotes'**.

POSITIONING WINDOWS ON THE SCREEN

Teach children to position their text editor window on the left and browser window on the right so they can make changes, save their file and preview it in the web browser by refreshing it.

Press the **'Refresh'** button to see changes. It may look like this: ⟳

Text editor – headings.html

```
<html>
  <h1>My short story</h1>
  <p>Once upon a time</p>
</html>
```

Try changing a few words. Then click **'File'** and **'Save'**.

Browser

//desktop/headings.html

My short story

Once upon a time

A MORE ADVANCED TEXT EDITOR

Children can use Notepad or TextEdit to start making HTML pages, but to progress with HTML and other web technologies, children need a more specialized text editor. A text editor that is designed to code in HTML will change the colour of keywords and check all tags have been typed properly. Sublime Text is a very useful text editor that can be downloaded and evaluated for free. Go to: **www.sublimetext.com**.

USEFUL HTML TAGS

TAG	WHAT IT DOES	EXAMPLE

`<html>...</html>`	Starts and ends an HTML file.	`<html>`
		`...`
		`</html>`

`<body>...</body>`	The body tag goes around the page content of an HTML file.	`<html>`
		`  <body>`
		`  ...`
		`  </body>`
		`</html>`

`<h1>...</h1>`
`<h2>...</h2>`
`<h6>...</h6>`
	Heading tags are used to make a heading. `<h1>` headings are the most important and therefore the biggest.	`<h1>My Page</h1>`

`<p>...</p>`	Paragraph tags are used to start and end a paragraph of text.	`<p>Once upon a time there was a monster. His name was Glug.</p>`
` `	The line break tag starts a new line in a web page.	`Line 1 Line 2`
`<a>...</a>`	The anchor tag is used to start and end a link, usually to another page.	`<a href="page2.html">Next page</a>`
`<img>`	The image tag is used to insert a picture or photo in a web page.	`<img src="dog.jpg">`
`<button>...</button>`	This puts a button on a page.	`<button>OK</button>`
`<title>...</title>`	The page title (shown in the browser bar) is set by using title tags.	`<title>This will show at the page top</title>`
`<strong>...</strong>`	Putting these tags around a word will make the word bold.	`It was an <strong>amazing</strong> day.`
`<em>...</em>`	Putting `<em>` and `</em>` around a word will make it italic.	`It was a <em>special</em> day.`
`<mark>...</mark>`	Putting `<mark>` and `</mark>` around a word will highlight it.	`You chose Yes <mark>No</mark>.`

The web pages in our books are made with minimal HTML to keep things simple. If children start creating pages to use online, they should begin each HTML file with **<!DOCTYPE html>** and use **<body>** and **<title>** tags.

COMMON PROBLEMS

1. The file type is wrong. Files must be saved as .html.

2. You're not working in 'plain text'. If you are using TextEdit on a Mac, make sure it is set to 'plain text' in 'Preferences'.

3. Smart quotes are not turned off. Make sure these are turned off in 'Preferences'. Quotes should be vertical and look like ' or " not ' or ".

4. The wrong file is open in the browser or it is not up to date. Sometimes children edit a file saved in one folder, but view one saved somewhere else in the browser.

Children must also make sure they save their file in the text editor and refresh the browser to see any changes.

5. Tags are misspelled or missing. Check they are correct! This is much easier in a dedicated HTML editor. Make sure there is a closing tag where appropriate (e.g. </script>).

6. Quotes or brackets are not matching. Make sure that there is a close bracket for every open bracket, and the same for every quote. Single quotes should match single quotes, and double match double quotes.

Styling with HTML

Book 4 gives children an overview of how to change the colour and style of objects on a web page. Large websites will do this with additional files containing CSS (Cascading Style Sheets). Here we use a simpler approach to explore the concept, by putting style attributes inside tags.

STYLE TAGS

To understand style tags, try the following code:

```
<html>
  <body style='background-color:yellow'>
    <h1 style='color:red'>Web</h1>
    <p style='color:green'>Internet</p>
  </body>
</html>
```

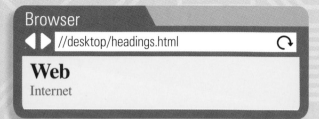

Style attributes can be combined by using semi-colons:

```
<p style='color:pink; text-align:left'>Hi</p>
```

HTML, JAVASCRIPT AND CSS

Most web pages use a combination of three languages or technologies: HTML, JavaScript and CSS.

HTML tells the browser what will go on a web page. It specifies what text, pictures, video and other objects will be shown. HTML can't do calculations or respond to inputs from the user, other than simple things like loading a new page.

JavaScript was designed to complement HTML by adding interactive functions so that objects on the web page can be changed, moved or hidden. JavaScript can do calculations, and is now a programming language in its own right.

CSS is used by designers to specify the appearance of what is shown to someone viewing the web page. It has become increasingly important as web pages are viewed on different-sized devices, from smart phones to large-screen TVs.

USEFUL HTML STYLE ATTRIBUTES		
STYLE ATTRIBUTE	**WHAT IT DOES**	**EXAMPLE**
background-color	Sets the background colour for an element in a web page.	background-color:red
color	Sets the colour for an element, some text for example.	color:blue
font-size	Sets the size for an element containing some text.	font-size:36px
font-family	Sets the font name for some text.	font-family:'Times New Roman'
text-align	Centres text, or justifies it to the left or right.	text-align:center
border-style	Creates a border around an HTML element.	border-style:dotted
padding	Makes some space between the edge of an element and what is inside it.	padding:10px

Where sizes are used, **px** means pixels. Note the American spellings of 'color' and 'center'.

After children have learnt to use HTML to create simple web pages, it is worth learning some JavaScript. JavaScript will allow children to control what happens when users click buttons or load a page, and make their pages much more interactive.

ADDING JAVASCRIPT

There are a number of different ways of adding JavaScript to a web page. In larger websites, JavaScript will be loaded from separate files. To give children a taste of the language, in this series we keep the JavaScript in the page, and use simple HTML event attributes to run code.

In the examples in Book 4, JavaScript is added in 2 ways:

1 Between **<script>** and **</script>** tags in an HTML page, which means it will run the script when the page loads.

2 Within an onclick HTML event attribute. For example:
<button onclick='alert("Hi")'>Press<button>

```
Remember:
HTML = what is on the page.
JavaScript = what the page does.
CSS = what the page looks like.
```

USEFUL JAVASCRIPT COMMANDS

COMMAND	WHAT IT DOES	EXAMPLE
alert()	Displays a message to the user.	alert('Hello world')
var	Defines a variable to be used.	var score=0
for	Makes a loop that repeats a number of times.	for(var n=0; n<10; n++)
document.write()	Adds something to the web page.	document.write(1)
document.writeln()	Adds something to the web page and starts a new line. (A **<pre>** tag also needs to be added to the web page.)	document.writeln(1)
if	Tests to see if a condition is true and runs code if it is.	if(age==10)alert('Ten')
else	If the condition is false, then runs some code.	else alert('You are not ten.')

function	Starts defining a function.	function sayHello()
		{
		   alert('Hello!')
		}

LANGUAGE COMPARISON

The four languages (or technologies) covered in this series – Logo, Scratch, Python and HTML/JavaScript – all play a part in helping children learn some of the key coding concepts. Each of the languages has its own strengths and weaknesses, and not all of them cover every concept.

It is helpful to compare how different languages approach similar concepts. This comparison will help children in two ways. First, it helps children think about the coding concept more deeply. Secondly, it helps them move from one language to another, allowing their learning to progress further.

LANGUAGES AND CONCEPTS

	LOGO	SCRATCH	PYTHON	HTML/JAVASCRIPT
Loops	`repeat 10 [ ... ]`	repeat 10	`for n in range(10):`	`for(var n=0;n<10;n++)`
Loop counter	`repeat 10 [print repcount]`	set a to 1 / repeat 10 / say n for 1 secs / change n by 1	`for n in range(1,11):` `    print(n)`	`for(var n=1;n<=10;n++)` `document.writeln(n);`

Selection	Not covered with Logo in this series.	ask Name? and wait / if answer = Ada then / say Hello!	`answer=input("name?")`
			`if answer=="Ada":`
			`    print("Hello!")`
				`var answer=prompt("Name?")`
				`if(answer=="Ada")`
				`    alert("Hello!")`

Structure*	Not covered with Logo in this series.	Drop all commands inside the 'C'.	`if answer=="Ada":`
			`    print("Hello!")`
			`    print("World!")`
			
			Indent lines of code with tabs.
				`if(answer=="Ada"){`
				`    alert("Hello!");`
				`    alert("World!");`
				`}`
				
				Put curly brackets {} around lines of code and a semi-colon at the end of a line.

Variables	Not covered with Logo in this series.	set a to 10 / change a by 20 / set a to a · 2	`a=10`
			
			`a=a+20`
			
			`a=a*2` Doubling a
				`var a=10;`
				
				`a=a+20;`
				
				`a=a*2;`
				
				The first time you use a variable, you need to declare it with **var**.

Random numbers	Not covered with Logo in this series.	pick random 1 to 6	`randint(1,6)` The random library needs to be imported first with **from random import ***	`parseInt(1+6*Math.random())`

Note that these are all short extracts of code. They need to be put in a program to be demonstrated.
*This is sometimes called indent style or bracketing. It describes the way different languages run multiple lines of code in a loop or after an 'if' command.

PROGRESSION STATEMENTS

All children learn at different rates. As they progress through this series of books and become better coders, there are a number of key concepts they need to understand and apply. This list will help children identify their own progress.

BOOK 1

☐ I understand that computers need instructions to do things.

☐ I know that instructions need to be precise.

☐ I know that instructions need to be given in the correct sequence.

☐ I can give instructions in Logo to move the turtle around the screen.

☐ I can give instructions in Scratch to move the sprite around the screen.

☐ I know that inputs are needed to change the way a program runs.

☐ I can make a program that uses a key press input to make a sprite move around.

☐ I can make my own simple program to move a sprite around the screen.

☐ I can debug my programs to spot and fix simple bugs.

BOOK 2

☐ I can explain what a loop is and why programs use them.

☐ I can program a 'repeat' loop in Logo or Scratch to draw a shape.

☐ I understand the difference between a loop that repeats a certain number of times and one that goes on forever.

☐ I can make a game that uses a 'repeat until' loop.

☐ I understand that sound is another output from a program and I can make a program that plays a sound.

☐ I understand what a variable is and how it can be used to keep the score in a game.

☐ I can make a game that uses a variable.

☐ I can debug my programs to fix some bugs.

BOOK 3

☐ I understand selection and what an 'if' command is.

☐ I can make a simple quiz using 'if' and 'else' commands.

☐ I can use Python to print messages on the screen and do simple calculations.

☐ I can use a 'for' loop to print a sequence of numbers.

☐ I understand what random numbers are, and can use them in simple programs.

☐ I can make my own simple game that uses loops, variables and 'if' commands.

☐ I can look through my code and work out where bugs are.

BOOK 4

☐ I understand that websites use HTML pages and how the internet connects computers together in a network.

☐ I can code a simple HTML page with different-sized headings and text.

☐ I can link pages together with anchor tags.

☐ I know how web pages call JavaScript when buttons are clicked or a web page loads.

☐ I can use JavaScript to make simple loops that print a sequence on a page.

☐ I can explain why making functions is a good idea.

☐ I can understand some messages I get from a debugging tool.

☐ I can make a mini web project linking several pages together and containing text and images.

ANSWERS

PAGE 9

1 48 clicks

2 5 clicks = move 96 steps, 2 clicks = move 240 steps. The screen is 480 steps wide.

Draws 1:

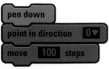

```
pen down
point in direction   0▼
move   100   steps
```

Draws 2:

```
pen down
point in direction   90▼
move   50   steps
turn ↻   90   degrees
move   50   steps
turn ↻   90   degrees
move   50   steps
turn ↺   90   degrees
move   50   steps
turn ↺   90   degrees
move   50   steps
```

Draws 3:

```
pen down
point in direction   90▼
move   50   steps
turn ↻   90   degrees
move   50   steps
turn ↻   90   degrees
move   50   steps
move   -50   steps
turn ↺   90   degrees
move   50   steps
turn ↻   90   degrees
move   50   steps
```

PAGE 10

1

```
when   up arrow ▼   key pressed
point in direction   0▼
move   10   steps
```
```
when   down arrow ▼   key pressed
point in direction   180▼
move   10   steps
```
```
when   left arrow ▼   key pressed
point in direction   -90▼
move   10   steps
```
```
when   right arrow ▼   key pressed
point in direction   90▼
move   10   steps
```

2

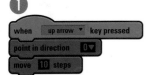

```
when   b ▼   key pressed
move   50   steps
```
```
when   s ▼   key pressed
move   2   steps
```

3

```
when   space ▼   key pressed
point in direction   45▼
move   10   steps
```

PAGE 11

1

```
when   c ▼   key pressed
clear
```

2

```
when   u ▼   key pressed
pen up
```

3

```
when   p ▼   key pressed
pen down
```

4

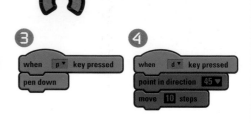

```
when   d ▼   key pressed
point in direction   45▼
move   10   steps
```

PAGE 16

1 repeat 72 [repeat 4 [fd 100 rt 90] rt 5]

PAGE 20

1 Edit the **'Change s by 1'** block to **'Change s by 2'**, **'Change s by 5'** or **'Change s by 10'**

PAGE 39

1 for(var n=0; n<41; n+=10)

2 for(var n=2; n<11; n+=2)

PAGE 47

1 **2**  **3**

PAGE 49

1, **2** and **3** are the same as page 47.

4 **5**

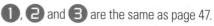

GLOSSARY

Algorithm The set of steps that solves a problem, or set of rules that defines a game or program.

Attributes Extra information about an object, such as its width or height.

Browser A program used to view websites and HTML pages. Popular browsers include Chrome, Internet Explorer, Firefox and Safari.

Command A word or code block that tells the computer what to do.

Coordinates The position of an object determined by its x (left to right) and y (bottom to top) values.

CSS (Cascading Style Sheets) The language used to store detailed style information for web pages.

Debugging Fixing problems (bugs) in a computer program.

Domain A part of the internet that is made up of computers or websites that are related in some way. For example, they may all be in the UK and have web addresses ending .co.uk.

Download To copy data from one computer to another using the internet.

Editor (or text editor) A program used to type and edit programs.

Embedding Including a video or map from another website within a web page.

Event Something that happens while a progam is running;, for example a key being pressed, or the program starting.

Function A sequence of commands created to do something such as draw a square every time the function is run or 'called'.

HTML (Hyper Text Mark-up Language) The language used to define the objects that are on web pages.

HTTP (Hyper Text Transfer Protocol) Rules for transporting HTML pages over the internet.

Hyperlink Link to another web page, which can be reached by clicking the mouse or touching a touchscreen.

IDLE The editor used to write Python code.

If...then...else A common form of selection in coding, where a command is run if something is true, and a different command if it is false.

Import To take data from one program into another.

Indent Using tabs or spaces to move a line of code in from the left.

Input An action (such as pressing a key) that tells a program to do something.

Integer A whole number. In code it means a type of variable that stores whole numbers.

Internet A worldwide network of computers.

JavaScript The programming language used in some web pages.

Language A system of words, numbers, symbols and rules for writing programs.

Library A collection of commands that are already stored and ready for use.

Listener (or event listener) A line of code or function that is only run when a particular event happens, such as a button being clicked.

Logo A computer language where commands move a turtle around the screen to draw.

Loop A sequence of commands repeated a number of times.

Main loop A loop in a game or program that contains the main part of the program.

Network A group of computers connected by wires or, often today, wireless links.

Online Connected to the internet.

Operator A piece of code that carries out a mathematical or logical operation.

Output Something that a computer program does to show the results of a program.

Parameter A value passed to a command. In the line of code fd(50), the parameter is 50.

Pixel A tiny dot on the screen of a computer or tablet.

Plain text Stored text that is all the same size, font and colour.

Program The special commands that tell a computer how to do something.

Python A text-based programming language.

Scratch A computer language that uses blocks to make a program.

Selection The way a computer program chooses which commands to run, after a simple question or value check.

Server A computer or group of computers that stores and delivers web pages.

Sprite An object moving around the screen.

String A sequence of letters or symbols. A string is a type of variable. A string can contain numbers but you cannot do mathematical operations in them.

Tags Special words and symbols used to describe what objects there are on a web page. They are always surrounded by angle brackets <>.

Turtle An onscreen robot that is moved around to draw in Logo or Python.

Upload To transfer files from your computer to another computer, which is often larger and in a different place.

URL (Uniform Resource Locator) The address or location of a website or HTML page. It is usually shown at the top of the browser window.

Variable A value or piece of data stored by a computer program.

Web page A page of information constructed using HTML and connected to the World Wide Web.

World Wide Web (or web) A worldwide network of HTML files, which we can access using the internet.

INDEX